D0728101

GIVE US
THIS DAY
OUR DAILY LOVE

GIVE US THIS DAY OUR DAILY LOVE

POPE FRANCIS ON THE FAMILY

Compiled by
Theresa Aletheia Noble, FSP
and Donna Giaimo, FSP

BOOKS & MEDIA
Boston

Library of Congress Cataloging-in-Publication Data

Catholic Church. Pope (2013- : Francis)
 [Dacci oggi il nostro amore quotidiano. English]
 Give us this day, our daily love : Pope Francis on the family / compiled by
Theresa Aletheia Noble, FSP, Donna Giaimo, FSP.
    pages cm
 Summary: "A collection of encouragement and inspiration for families from
Pope Francis"-- Provided by publisher.
 ISBN 978-0-8198-3135-4 (pbk.) -- ISBN 0-8198-3135-2 (pbk.)
 1. Families--Religious aspects--Catholic Church. I. Francis, Pope, 1936- II.
Noble, Theresa, compiler. III. Title.
 BX2351.C38513 2015
 248.4'82--dc23
                          2014042844

Unless otherwise noted, the Scripture quotations contained herein are taken directly from Pope Francis' works.

Original material from Pope Francis' audiences, homilies, angelus messages, addresses, encyclicals, letters, and exhortations copyright © Libreria Editrice Vaticana, 00120 Città del Vaticano. Used with permission.

Cover design by Rosana Usselmann

Cover photo by Stefano Spaziani

All rights reserved. No part of this book may be reproduced or transmitted in any form or by any means, electronic or mechanical, including photocopying, recording, or by any information storage and retrieval system, without permission in writing from the publisher.

"P" and PAULINE are registered trademarks of the Daughters of St. Paul.

Copyright © 2015, Daughters of St. Paul

Published by Pauline Books & Media, 50 Saint Pauls Avenue, Boston, MA 02130–3491

Printed in the U.S.A.

www.pauline.org

Pauline Books & Media is the publishing house of the Daughters of St. Paul, an international congregation of women religious serving the Church with the communications media.

23456789   21 20 19 18 17

Contents

Prayer to the Holy Family

Jesus, Mary, and Joseph,
in you we contemplate
the splendor of true love;
to you we turn with trust.
Holy Family of Nazareth,
grant that our families too
may be places of communion and prayer,
authentic schools of the Gospel
and small domestic Churches.

Holy Family of Nazareth,
may families never again
experience violence, rejection, and division:
may all who have been hurt or scandalized
find ready comfort and healing.

Holy Family of Nazareth,
may the Synod of Bishops

make us once more mindful
of the sacredness and inviolability of the family,
and its beauty in God's plan.

Jesus, Mary, and Joseph,
graciously hear our prayer.

Angelus message, December 29, 2013

The Sacrament of Marriage

"Marriage is the icon of God's love for us."

Created in Order to Love

The image of God is the married couple: the man and the woman; not only the man, not only the woman, but both of them together. This is the image of God: love; God's covenant with us is represented in that covenant between man and woman. And this is very beautiful! We are created in order to love, as a reflection of God and his love. And in the marital union man and woman fulfill this vocation through their mutual reciprocity and their full and definitive communion of life.

When a man and woman celebrate the Sacrament of Matrimony, God as it were "is mirrored" in them; he impresses in them his own features and the indelible character of his love. Marriage is the icon of God's love for us. Indeed, God is communion too: the three Persons of the Father, the Son, and the Holy Spirit live eternally in perfect unity. And this is precisely the mystery of Matrimony: God makes of the two spouses one single life. The Bible uses a powerful expression and says "one flesh," so intimate is the union between man and woman in marriage. And this is precisely the mystery of marriage: the love of God which is reflected in the couple that decides to live together. Therefore a man leaves his home, the home of his parents, and goes to live with his wife and unites himself so strongly to her that the two become—the Bible says—one flesh.

There is a truly marvelous design inherent in the Sacrament of Matrimony! And it unfolds in the simplicity and frailty of the human condition. We are well aware of how many difficulties two spouses experience. . . . The important thing is to keep alive their bond with God, who stands as the foundation of the marital bond. And the true bond is always the Lord. When the family prays, the bond is preserved. When the husband prays for his wife and the wife prays for her husband, that bond becomes strong; one praying for the other. It is true that there are so many difficulties in married life, so many, when there is insufficient work or money, when the children have problems. So much to contend with. And many times the husband and wife become a little fractious and argue between themselves. They argue; this is how it is. There is always arguing in marriage; sometimes the plates even fly. Yet we must not become saddened by this; this is the human condition. The secret is that love is stronger than the moment when there is arguing, and therefore I always advise spouses: do not let a day when you have argued end without making peace. Always! And to make peace it isn't necessary to call the United Nations to

> "When a man and woman celebrate the Sacrament of Matrimony, God as it were 'is mirrored' in them..."

come to the house and make peace. A little gesture is sufficient, a caress, and then let it be! Until tomorrow! And tomorrow begin again. And this is life, carrying on, carrying on with courage and the desire to live together. And this is truly great; it is beautiful!

General Audience, April 2, 2014

Renewing the Sacrament of Marriage

The family is founded on marriage. Through their free and faithful act of love, Christian spouses testify to the fact that marriage, insofar as it is a sacrament, is the foundation of the family and strengthens spousal union and the couple's mutual gift of self. It is as though matrimony were first a human sacrament, where the person discovers himself, understands himself in relation to others and in a relationship of love which is capable of receiving and giving. Spousal and familial love also clearly reveals the vocation of the person to love in a unique way and forever, and that the trials, sacrifices, and crises of couples as well as of the family as a whole represent pathways for growth in goodness, truth, and beauty. In marriage we give ourselves completely without calculation or reserve, sharing everything, gifts and hardship, trusting in God's Providence. This is the experience that the young can learn from their parents and grandparents. It is an experience of faith in God and of mutual trust, profound freedom, and holiness, because holiness presumes giving oneself with fidelity and sacrifice every day of one's life! But there are problems in marriage. Always different points of view, jealousy, arguing. But we need to say to young spouses that they should never end the day without making peace. The Sacrament of Marriage is renewed in this act of peace after an argument, a misunderstanding, a hidden jealousy, even a sin. Making peace gives unity to the family; and tell young people, young couples, that it is not easy to go down this path, but it is a very beautiful path, very beautiful. You need to tell them!

"In marriage we give ourselves completely without calculation or reserve, sharing everything, gifts and hardship, trusting in God's Providence."

Address to the participants in the plenary assembly of the Pontifical Council for the Family, October 25, 2013

Building a Forever Home

It's important to ask yourself if it is possible to love each other "forever." This is a question that must be asked: Is it possible to love "forever"? Today so many people are afraid of making definitive decisions. One boy said to his bishop: "I want to become a priest, but only for ten years." He was afraid of a definitive choice. But that is a general fear that comes from our culture. To make life decisions seems impossible. Today everything changes so quickly, nothing lasts long. And this mentality leads many who are preparing for marriage to say: "We are together as long as the love lasts"; and then? All the best and see you later . . . and so ends the marriage. But what do we mean by "love"? Is it only a feeling, a psychophysical state? Certainly, if that is it, then we cannot build on anything solid. But if, instead, love is a relationship, then it is a reality that grows, and we can also say by way of example that it is built up like a home. And a home is built together, not alone! To build something here means to foster and aid growth.

Dear engaged couples, you are preparing to grow together, to build this home, to live together forever. You do not want to found it on the sand of sentiments, which come and go, but on the rock of true love, the love that comes from God. The family is born from this plan of love; it wants to grow just as a home is built, as a place of affection, of help, of hope, of support.

> "This is a question that must be asked: Is it possible to love 'forever'?"

As the love of God is stable and forever, so too should we want the love on which a family is based to be stable and forever. Please, we mustn't let ourselves be overcome by the "culture of the provisory"! Today this culture invades us all, this culture of the temporary. This is not right!

Address to engaged couples, February 14, 2014

Give Us This Day
Our Daily Love

How, then, does one cure this fear of the "forever"? One cures it day by day, by entrusting oneself to the Lord Jesus in a life that becomes a daily spiritual journey, made in steps—little steps, steps of shared growth. It is accomplished through a commitment to becoming men and women who are mature in faith. For, dear engaged couples, "forever" is not only a question of duration! A marriage is not successful just because it endures; quality is important. To stay together and to know how to love one another forever is the challenge for Christian couples. What comes to mind is the miracle of the multiplication of the loaves: for you, too, the Lord can multiply your love and give it to you fresh and good each day. He has an infinite reserve! He gives you the love that stands at the foundation of your union and each day he renews and strengthens it. And he makes it ever greater when the family grows with children.

On this journey prayer is important; it is necessary, always: he for her, she for him, and both together. Ask Jesus to multiply your love. In the prayer of the Our Father we say: "Give us this day our daily bread." Spouses can also learn to pray like this: "Lord, give us this day our daily love," for the daily love of spouses is bread, the true bread of the soul, what sustains them in going forward. And the prayer: can we practice to see if we know how to say it? "Lord, give us this day our daily love." All together! [Couples: "Lord, give us this day our daily love."] One more time! [Couples: "Lord, give us this day our daily love."] This is the prayer for engaged couples and spouses. Teach us to love one another, to will good to the other! The more you trust in him, the more your love will be "forever"— able to be renewed—and it will conquer every difficulty.

> "A marriage is not successful just because it endures; quality is important."

Address to engaged couples, February 14, 2014

Restored in Christ's Love

The love of Christ, which has blessed and sanctified the union of husband and wife, is able to sustain their love and to renew it when, humanly speaking, it becomes lost, wounded, or worn out. The love of Christ can restore to spouses the joy of journeying together. This is what marriage is all about: man and woman walking together, wherein the husband helps his wife to become ever more a woman, and wherein the woman has the task of helping her husband to become ever more a man. This is the task that you both share. "I love you, and for this love I help you to become ever more a woman"; "I love you, and for this love I help you to become ever more a man." Here we see the reciprocity of differences. The path is not always a smooth one, free of disagreements, otherwise it would not be human. It is a demanding journey, at times difficult and at times turbulent, but such is life! Within this theology which the word of God offers us concerning the people on a journey, spouses on a journey, I would like to give you some advice. It is normal for husband and wife to argue: it's normal. It always happens. But my advice is this: never let the day end without having first made peace. Never! A small gesture is sufficient. Thus the journey may continue. Marriage is a symbol of life, real life: it is not "fiction"! It is the Sacrament of the love of Christ and the Church, a love which finds its proof and guarantee in the cross. My desire for you is that you have a good journey, a fruitful one, growing in love. I wish you happiness. There will be crosses! But the Lord is always there to help us move forward. May the Lord bless you!

> "Marriage is a symbol of life, real life: it is not 'fiction'! It is the Sacrament of the love of Christ and the Church...."

Homily, September 14, 2014

Hand in Hand, Always

Those who celebrate the Sacrament [of Marriage] say, *"I promise to be true to you, in joy and in sadness, in sickness and in health; I will love you and honor you all the days of my life."* At that moment, the couple does not know what will happen, nor what joys and pains await them. They are setting out, like Abraham, on a journey together. And that is what marriage is! Setting out and walking together, hand in hand, putting yourselves in the Lord's powerful hands. Hand in hand, always and for the rest of your lives. And do not pay attention to this makeshift culture, which can shatter our lives.

With trust in God's faithfulness, everything can be faced responsibly and without fear. Christian spouses are not naïve; they know life's problems and temptations. But they are not afraid to be responsible before God and before society. They do not run away, they do not hide, they do not shirk the mission of forming a family and bringing children into the world. "But today, Father, it is difficult. . . . " Of course it is difficult! That is why we need the grace, the grace that comes from the sacrament! The sacraments are not decorations in life—what a beautiful marriage, what a beautiful ceremony, what a beautiful banquet. . . . But that is not the Sacrament of Marriage. That is a decoration! Grace is not given to decorate life but rather to make us strong in life, giving us courage to go forward! And without isolating oneself but always staying together.

Address to the participants in the Pilgrimage of
Families during the Year of Faith, October 26, 2013

Source of Strength and Joy

Christians celebrate the Sacrament of Marriage because they know they need it! They need it to stay together and to carry out their mission as parents. "In joy and in sadness, in sickness and in health." This is what the spouses say to one another during the celebration of the sacrament, and in their marriage they pray with one another and with the community. Why? Because it is helpful to do so? No! They do so because they need to, for the long journey they are making together; it is a long journey, not for a brief spell but for an entire life! And they need Jesus' help to walk beside one another in trust, to accept one another each day, and daily to forgive one another. And this is important! To know how to forgive one another in families because we all make mistakes, all of us! Sometimes we do things which are not good and which harm others. It is important to have the courage to ask for forgiveness when we are at fault in the family. Some weeks ago, in this very square, I said that in order to have a healthy family, three words need to be used. And I want to repeat these three words:

please, thank you, sorry. Three essential words! We say please so as not to be forceful in family life: "May I please do this? Would you be happy if I did this?" We do this with a language that seeks agreement. We say thank you, thank you for love! But be honest with me, how many times do you say thank you to your wife, and you to your husband? How many days go by without uttering this word: thanks! And the last word: sorry. We all make mistakes and on occasion someone gets offended in the marriage, in the family, and sometimes—I say—plates are smashed, harsh words are spoken, but please listen to my advice: don't ever let the sun set without reconciling. Peace is made each day in the family: "Please forgive me," and then you start over. Please, thank you, sorry! Shall we say them together? [All reply "yes."] Please, thank you, and sorry. Let us say these words in our families! To forgive one another each day!

> "It is important to have the courage to ask for forgiveness when we are at fault in the family."

The life of a family is filled with beautiful moments: rest, meals together, walks in the park or the countryside, visits to grandparents or to a sick person. . . . But if love is missing, joy is missing, nothing is fun. Jesus always gives us that love; he is its endless source. In the sacrament he gives us his word and he gives us the Bread of Life, so that our joy may be complete.

Address to the participants in the Pilgrimage
of Families during the Year of Faith, October 26, 2013

Marriage Takes Courage

What a beautiful witness! Two young people who have chosen, who have joyfully and courageously decided to form a family. Yes, it is so true that it takes courage to form a family. It takes courage! . . .

What is marriage? It is a true and authentic vocation, as are the priesthood and the religious life. Two Christians who marry have recognized the call of the Lord in their own love story, the vocation to form one flesh and one life from two, male and female. And the Sacrament of Holy Matrimony envelops this love in the grace of God; it roots it in God himself. By this gift, and by the certainty of this call, you can continue on assured; you have nothing to fear; you can face everything together!

Let us think about our parents, about our grandparents and great-grandparents: they married in much poorer conditions than our own. Some married during wartime or just after a war. Some, like my own parents, emigrated. Where did they find the strength? They found it in the certainty that the Lord was with them, that their families were blessed by God through the Sacrament of Matrimony, and that the mission of bringing children into the world and educating them is also blessed. With this assurance they overcame even the most difficult trials. These were simple certainties, but they were real; they were the pillars that supported their love. Their lives were not easy; there were problems, many, many problems. However, these simple assurances helped them to go forward. And they succeeded in having beautiful families and in giving life and in raising their children.

> "And the Sacrament of Holy Matrimony envelops this love in the grace of God; it roots it in God himself."

Dear friends, this moral and spiritual foundation is necessary in order to build well in a lasting way! Today, this foundation is no longer guaranteed by family life and the social tradition. Indeed, the society in which you were raised favors individual rights rather than the family—these individual rights. It favors relationships that last until difficulties arise, and this is why it sometimes speaks about relationships between couples, within families, and between spouses in a superficial and misleading way. It is enough to watch certain television programs to see these values on display! How many times parish priests—sometimes I myself also heard it—hear a couple that comes to get married say: "Ah, we love each other so much, but . . . we'll stay together as long as the love lasts. When it ends, we'll each go our separate way." This is selfishness: when I feel like it, I'll end the marriage and forget the "one flesh" that cannot be separated. It is risky to get married; it is risky! It is this egoism which threatens it, because we each have within us this possibility of a dual personality: the one that says, "I am free, I want this . . . " and the other which says, "I, me, to me, with me, for me. . . . " Selfishness always returns and does not know how to open up to others. The other difficulty is this culture of the temporary: it seems as though nothing is definitive. Everything is provisional. As I said before: love, as long as it lasts. . . . Jesus didn't save us temporarily; he saved us definitively!

Do not be afraid to take steps which are permanent, like getting married; deepen your love by respecting its seasons and expressions, pray, prepare yourselves well, and then trust that the Lord will not leave you alone! Let him come into your home like one of the family; he will always sustain you!

Address to the young people of Umbria gathered in the square in front of the Basilica of Saint Mary of the Angels, Assisi, October 4, 2013

The Vocation of Love

I n Abraham's journey toward the future city, the Letter to the Hebrews mentions the blessing which was passed on from fathers to sons (cf. Heb 11:20–21). The first setting in which faith enlightens the human city is the family. I think first and foremost of the stable union of man and woman in marriage. This union is born of their love, as a sign and presence of God's own love, and of the acknowledgment and acceptance of the goodness of sexual differentiation, whereby spouses can become one flesh (cf. Gen 2:24) and are enabled to give birth to a new life, a manifestation of the Creator's goodness, wisdom, and loving plan. Grounded in this love, a man and a woman can promise each other mutual love in a gesture which engages their entire lives and mirrors many features of faith. Promising love forever is possible when we perceive a plan bigger than our own ideas and undertakings, a plan which sustains us and enables us to surrender our future entirely to the one we love. Faith also helps us to grasp in all its depth and richness the begetting of children, as a sign of the love of the Creator who entrusts us with the mystery of a new person. So it was that Sarah, by faith, became a mother, for she trusted in God's fidelity to his promise (cf. Heb 11:11).

In the family, faith accompanies every age of life, beginning with childhood: children learn to trust in the love of their parents. This is why it is so important that within their families parents encourage shared expressions of faith which can help children gradually to mature in their own faith. Young people in particular, who are going through a period in their lives which is so complex, rich, and important for their faith, ought to feel the constant closeness and support of their families and the Church in their journey of faith. We have all seen, during World Youth Days, the joy that young people show in their faith and their desire for an ever more solid and generous life of faith. Young people want to live life to the fullest. Encountering Christ, letting themselves be caught up in and guided by his love, enlarges the horizons of existence, gives it a firm hope which will not disappoint. Faith is no refuge for the fainthearted, but something which enhances our lives. It makes us aware of a magnificent calling, the vocation of love. It assures us that this love is trustworthy and worth embracing, for it is based on God's faithfulness which is stronger than our every weakness.

> "Promising love forever is possible when we perceive a plan bigger than our own ideas and undertakings…"

Encyclical Letter Lumen Fidei
(nos. 52–53), June 29, 2013

The Masterpiece of Creation

The creation of man and woman is the masterpiece of creation. [God] did not want for man to be alone: he wanted him to be with his companion, his companion on the journey.

... The Lord holds up this love contained in the masterpiece of creation in order to explain the love he has for his people. Yet there is another step: when Paul needs to explain the mystery of Christ, he also does so in relation and in reference to the bride. For Christ is wedded: he wedded the Church, his people; as the Father had wedded his people Israel, so Christ espoused his people to himself.

This is the story of love. This is the story of the masterpiece of creation. And casuistry crumbles before this journey of love, before this icon, and becomes pain. ... When [a man] leaves his father and mother to be joined to a woman, when they become one flesh and continue on, when this love fails—for it often fails—we need to feel the pain of the failure. [We also need] to accompany those persons who have failed in their love. [Not] to condemn [but] to walk with them. . . .

The journey of love of Christian marriage, which God blessed in the masterpiece of his creation with a blessing that can never be taken away. Not even original sin destroyed it. . . . How beautiful love is, how beautiful marriage is, how beautiful the family is, how beautiful this journey is. [But] how much love, and what great closeness we should also have for our brothers and sisters who, in their lives, have had the misfortune of a failed love.

" . . . when this love fails—for it often fails—we need to feel the pain of the failure."

Homily, February 28, 2014

Repeating Our "Yes" Every Day

God surprises us with his love, but he demands that we be faithful in following him. We can be unfaithful, but he cannot: he is "the faithful one," and he demands of us that same fidelity. Think of all the times when we were excited about something or other, some initiative, some task, but afterward, at the first sign of difficulty, we threw in the towel. Sadly, this also happens in the case of fundamental decisions such as marriage. It is the difficulty of remaining steadfast, faithful to decisions we have made and to commitments we have made. Often it is easy enough to say "yes," but then we fail to repeat this "yes" each and every day. We fail to be faithful.

Mary said her "yes" to God: a "yes" which threw her simple life in Nazareth into turmoil, and not only once. Any number of times she had to utter a heartfelt "yes" at moments of joy and sorrow, culminating in the "yes" she spoke at the foot of the cross. Here today there are many mothers present; think of the full extent of Mary's faithfulness to God: seeing her only Son hanging on the cross. The faithful woman, still standing, utterly heartbroken, yet faithful and strong.

And I ask myself: Am I a Christian by fits and starts, or am I a Christian full-time? Our culture of the ephemeral, the relative, also takes its toll on the way we live our faith. God asks us to be faithful to him, daily, in our everyday life. He goes on to say that, even if we are sometimes unfaithful to him, he remains faithful. In his mercy, he never tires of stretching out his hand to lift us up, to encourage us to continue our journey, to come back and tell him of our weakness, so that he can grant us his strength. This is the real journey: to walk with the Lord always, even at moments of weakness, even in our sins. Never to prefer a makeshift path of our own. That kills us. Faith is ultimate fidelity, like that of Mary.

> "Often it is easy enough to say 'yes,' but then we fail to repeat this 'yes' each and every day."

Homily, October 13, 2013

Nurturing Family Life

"In your journey as a family,
you share so many beautiful moments."

Family: Hope and Future

For the Christian community the family is far more than a "theme": it is life, it is the daily fabric of life, it is the journey of generations who pass on the faith together with love and with the basic moral values. It is concrete solidarity, effort, patience, and also a project, hope, a future. All this which the Christian community lives out in the light of faith, hope, and charity should never be kept to oneself but must become, every day, the leaven in the dough of the whole of society for its greater common good. . . .

The family is the privileged school for learning generosity, sharing, responsibility; a school that teaches how to overcome a certain individualistic mindset which has worked its way into our societies. Sustaining and promoting families, making the most of their fundamental and central role, means working for a just and supportive development.

We cannot ignore the hardship of many families that is due to unemployment, the problem of housing, the practical impossibility of freely choosing their own educational curriculum; the suffering that is also due to internal conflicts within families, to the failures of the conjugal and family experience, and to the violence that unfortunately lurks in families and wreaks havoc even in our homes. We owe it to all and wish to be particularly close to them with respect and with a true sense of brotherhood and solidarity. However, we want above all to remember the simple but beautiful and brave testimony of so many families who joyfully live the experience of marriage and parenthood enlightened and sustained by the Lord's grace and fearlessly face even moments of the cross. Lived in union with the cross of the Lord, the cross does not hinder the path of love but on the contrary can make it stronger and fuller.

"The family is the privileged school for learning generosity, sharing, responsibility…"

Address to the 47th Social Week of Italian Catholics, September 11, 2013

Spend Time Together

L et me tell you one thing: when I [hear confessions]—now not as often as when I was in the other diocese—when a young mom or dad comes, I ask: "How many children do you have?" and they tell me. And I always ask another question: "Tell me: do you play with your children?" Most of them answer: "What are you asking, Father?"—"Yes, yes: do you play? Do you spend time with your children?" We are losing this capacity, this wisdom of playing with our children. The economic situation pushes us to this, to lose this. Please, spend time with our children! . . . This is a "crucial" point, a point which allows us to discern, to evaluate the human quality of the present economic system. And found within this context is also the issue of working Sundays, which concerns not only believers, but touches everyone, as an ethical choice. It is this area of gratuitousness that we are losing. The question is: "What do we want to give priority to?" Having Sundays free from work—apart from necessary services—stands to confirm that the priority is not economic but human, gratuitousness, not business relationships but those of family, of friends, for believers the relationship with God and with the community. Perhaps we have reached the moment to ask ourselves whether working on Sunday is true freedom. Because the God of surprises and the God who breaks molds surprises and breaks molds so that we may become more free; he is the God of freedom.

Address to workers during a pastoral visit to the dioceses of Campobasso-Boiano and Isernia-Venafro, July 5, 2014

Where Is My Heart?

We all have desires. The poor ones are those who have no desire, no desire to go forward, toward the horizon; and for us Christians this horizon is the encounter with Jesus, the very encounter with him who is our life, our joy, our happiness. I would like to ask you two questions. First: Do you all have a desiring heart? A heart that desires? Think about it and respond silently in your hearts. I ask you: Is your heart filled with desire, or is it a closed heart, a sleeping heart, a heart numb to the things of life? The desire to go forward to encounter Jesus. The second question: Where is your treasure, what are you longing for? Jesus told us: Where your treasure is, there will be your heart—and I ask you: Where is your treasure? What is the most important reality for you, the most precious reality, the one that attracts your heart like a magnet? What attracts your heart? May I say that it is God's love? Do you wish to do good to others, to live for the Lord and for your brothers and sisters? May I say this? Each one answer in his own heart. But someone could tell me: Father, I am someone who works, who has a family; for me the most important reality is to keep my family and work going. . . . Certainly, this is true, it is important. But what is the power that unites the family? It is indeed love, and the One who sows love in our hearts is God, God's love; it is precisely God's love that gives meaning to our small daily tasks and helps us face the great trials. This is the true treasure of humankind: going forward in life with love, with that love which the Lord has sown in our hearts, with God's love. This is the true treasure. But what is God's love? It is not something vague, some generic feeling. God's love has a name and a face: Jesus Christ, Jesus. Love for God is made manifest in Jesus. For we cannot love air. . . . Do we love air? Do we love all things? No, no we cannot, we love people and the person we love is Jesus, the gift of the Father among us. It is a love that gives value and beauty to everything else; a love that gives strength to the family, to work, to study, to friendship, to art, to all human activity. It even gives meaning to negative experiences, because this love allows us to move beyond these experiences, to go beyond them, not to remain prisoners of evil; it moves us beyond, always opening us to hope, that's it! Love of God in Jesus always opens us to hope, to that horizon of hope, to the final horizon of our pilgrimage.

> " . . . it is precisely God's love that gives meaning to our small daily tasks and helps us face the great trials."

Angelus message, August 11, 2013

Prayer Gives Strength

The family prays. The Gospel passage speaks about two ways of praying; one is false—that of the Pharisee—and the other is authentic: that of the tax collector. The Pharisee embodies an attitude which does not express thanksgiving to God for his blessings and his mercy, but rather self-satisfaction. The Pharisee feels himself justified, he feels his life is in order, he boasts of this, and he judges others from his pedestal. The tax collector, on the other hand, does not multiply words. His prayer is humble, sober, pervaded by a consciousness of his own unworthiness, of his own needs. Here is a man who truly realizes that he needs God's forgiveness and his mercy.

The prayer of the tax collector is the prayer of the poor man, a prayer pleasing to God. It is a prayer which, as the first reading says, "will reach to the clouds" (Sir 35:20), unlike the prayer of the Pharisee, which is weighed down by vanity.

In the light of God's word, I would like to ask you, dear families: Do you pray together from time to time as a family? Some of you do, I know. But so many people say to me: But how can we? As the tax collector does, it is clear: humbly, before God. Each one, with humility, allowing themselves to be gazed upon by the Lord and imploring his goodness, that he may visit us. But in the family how is this done? After all, prayer seems to be something personal, and besides there is never a good time, a moment of peace. . . . Yes, all that is true enough, but it is also a matter of humility, of realizing that we need God, like the tax collector! And all families—we need God: all of us! We need his help, his strength, his blessing, his mercy, his forgiveness. And

> "Praying the Our Father together, around the table, is not something extraordinary: it's easy."

we need simplicity to pray as a family: simplicity is necessary! Praying the Our Father together, around the table, is not something extraordinary: it's easy. And praying the Rosary together, as a family, is very beautiful and a source of great strength! And also praying for one another! The husband for his wife, the wife for her husband, both together for their children, the children for their grandparents . . . praying for each other. This is what it means to pray in the family and it is what makes the family strong: prayer.

Homily for the Family Day
during the Year of Faith, October 27, 2013

The Joy of Faith

The family experiences joy. In the responsorial psalm we find these words: "let the humble hear and be glad" (33/34:2). The entire psalm is a hymn to the Lord who is the source of joy and peace. What is the reason for this gladness? It is that the Lord is near, he hears the cry of the lowly and he frees them from evil. As Saint Paul himself writes: "Rejoice always.... The Lord is near" (Phil 4:4–5). I would like to ask you all a question today. But each of you keep it in your heart and take it home. You can regard it as a kind of "homework." Only you must answer. How are things when it comes to joy at home? Is there joy in your family? You can answer this question.

Dear families, you know very well that the true joy which we experience in the family is not superficial; it does not come from material objects, from the fact that everything seems to be going well.... True joy comes from a profound harmony between persons, something which we all feel in our hearts and which makes us experience the beauty of togetherness, of mutual support along life's journey. But the basis of this feeling of deep joy is the presence of God, the presence of God in the family and his love, which is welcoming, merciful, and respectful toward all. And above all a love which is patient; patience is a virtue of God and he teaches us how to cultivate it in family life, how to be patient, and lovingly so, with each other. To be patient among ourselves. A patient love. God alone knows how to create harmony from differences. But if God's love is lacking, the family loses its harmony; self-centeredness prevails and joy fades. But the family which experiences the joy of faith communicates it naturally. That family is the salt of the earth and the light of the world, it is the leaven of society as a whole.

Dear families, always live in faith and simplicity, like the Holy Family of Nazareth! The joy and peace of the Lord be always with you!

Homily for the Family Day
during the Year of Faith, October 27, 2013

> "True joy comes from a profound harmony between persons, something which we all feel in our hearts and which makes us experience the beauty of togetherness, of mutual support along life's journey."

Praying the Rosary

In the silence of the daily routine, Saint Joseph, together with Mary, share a single common center of attention: Jesus. They accompany and nurture the growth of the Son of God made man for us with commitment and tenderness, reflecting on everything that happened. In the Gospels, Saint Luke twice emphasizes the attitude of Mary, which is also that of Saint Joseph: she "kept all these things, pondering them in her heart" (2:19, 51). To listen to the Lord, we must learn to contemplate, feel his constant presence in our lives, and we must stop and converse with him, give him space in prayer. Each of us, even you boys and girls, young people, so many of you here this morning, should ask yourselves: "How much space do I give to the Lord? Do I stop to talk with him?" Ever since we were children, our parents have taught us to start and end the day with a prayer, to teach us to feel that the friendship and the love of God accompanies us. Let us remember the Lord more in our daily life!

And in this month of May, I would like to recall the importance and beauty of the prayer of the Holy Rosary. Reciting the Hail Mary, we are led to contemplate the mysteries of Jesus, that is, to reflect on the key moments of his life, so that, as with Mary and Saint Joseph, he is the center of our thoughts, of our attention and our actions. It would be nice if, especially in this month of May, we could pray the Holy Rosary together in the family, with friends, in the parish, or some prayer to Jesus and the Virgin Mary! Praying together is a precious moment that further strengthens family life, friendship! Let us learn to pray more in the family and as a family!

General Audience, May 1, 2013

"Ever since we were children, our parents have taught us to start and end the day with a prayer, to teach us to feel that the friendship and the love of God accompanies us."

The Dignity of Work

In the Gospel of Saint Matthew, in one of the moments when Jesus returns to his town, to Nazareth, and speaks in the Synagogue, the amazement of his fellow townspeople at his wisdom is emphasized. They asked themselves the question: "Is not this the carpenter's son?" (13:55) Jesus comes into our history; he comes among us by being born of Mary by the power of God, but with the presence of Saint Joseph, the legal father who cares for him and also teaches him his trade. Jesus is born and lives in a family, in the Holy Family, learning the carpenter's craft from Saint Joseph in his workshop in Nazareth, sharing with him the commitment, effort, satisfaction, and also the difficulties of every day.

This reminds us of the dignity and importance of work. The Book of Genesis tells us that God created man and woman, entrusting them with the task of filling the earth and subduing it, which does not mean exploiting it but nurturing and protecting it, caring for it through their work (cf. Gen 1:28; 2:15). Work is part of God's loving plan; we are called to cultivate and care for all the goods of creation and in this way share in the work of creation! Work is fundamental to the dignity of a person. Work, to use a metaphor, "anoints" us with dignity, fills us with dignity, [and] makes us similar to God, who has worked and still works, who always acts (cf. Jn 5:17); it gives one the ability to maintain oneself, one's family, to contribute to the growth of one's own nation. And here I think of the difficulties which, in various countries, afflict the world of work and business today; I am thinking of how many, and not only young people, are unemployed, often due to a purely economic conception of society, which seeks profit selfishly, beyond the parameters of social justice.

> "Work, to use a metaphor, 'anoints' us with dignity, fills us with dignity, [and] makes us similar to God, who has worked and still works…"

I wish to extend an invitation to solidarity to everyone, and I would like to encourage those in public office to make every effort to give new impetus to employment; this means caring for the dignity of the person, but above all I would say do not lose hope. Saint Joseph also experienced moments of difficulty, but he never lost faith and was able to overcome them, in the certainty that God never abandons us. And then I would like to speak especially to you young people: be committed to your daily duties, your studies, your work; to relationships of friendship; to helping others; your future also depends on how you live these precious years of your life. Do not be afraid of commitment, of sacrifice, and do not view the future with fear. Keep your hope alive; there is always a light on the horizon.

General Audience, May 1, 2013

What Is in My Heart?

One time, the disciples of Jesus were eating grain because they were hungry; but it was Saturday and on Saturday grain was not allowed to be eaten. Still, they picked it and ate the grain. And [the Pharisees] said: "But look at what they are doing! Whoever does this breaks the Law and soils his soul, for he does not obey the Law!" And Jesus responded: "Nothing that comes from without soils the soul. Only what comes from within, from your heart, can soil your soul." And I believe that it would do us good today to think not about whether my soul is clean or dirty, but rather about what is in my heart, what I have inside, what I know I have but no one else knows. Being honest with yourself is not easy, because we always try to cover it up when we see something wrong inside, no? . . . What is in our heart; is it love? Let us think: Do I love my parents, my children, my wife, my husband, people in the neighborhood, the sick? . . . Do I love? Is there hate? Do I hate someone? Often we find hatred, don't we? "I love everyone except for this one, this one, and that one!" That's hatred, isn't it? What is in my heart: forgiveness? Is there an attitude of forgiveness for those who have offended me, or is there an attitude of revenge? "He will pay for it!" We must ask ourselves what is within, because what is inside comes out and harms, if it is evil; and if it is good, it comes out and does good. And it is so beautiful to tell ourselves the truth and feel ashamed when we are in a situation that is not what God wants, it is not good; when my heart feels hatred, revenge, so many situations are sinful. How is my heart? . . .

> "And I believe that it would do us good today to think not about whether my soul is clean or dirty, but rather about what is in my heart, what I have inside . . ."

Homily at the Roman parish of
Saint Thomas the Apostle, February 16, 2014

Fathers and Mothers

*"We must reaffirm the right of children to grow up in a family
with a father and a mother capable of creating
a suitable environment for the child's
development and emotional maturity."*

The Greatness of Joseph's Heart

Joseph and Mary were dwelling in Nazareth; they were not yet living together, because they were not yet married. In the meantime, Mary, after having welcomed the Angel's announcement, came to be with child by the power of the Holy Spirit. When Joseph realized this, he was bewildered. The Gospel does not explain what his thoughts were, but it does tell us the essential: he seeks to do the will of God and is ready for the most radical renunciation. Rather than defending himself and asserting his rights, Joseph chooses what for him is an enormous sacrifice. And the Gospel tells us: "Joseph, being a just man and unwilling to put her to shame, resolved to send her away quietly" (1:19).

This brief sentence reveals a true inner drama if we think about the love that Joseph had for Mary! But even in these circumstances, Joseph intends to do the will of God and decides, surely with great sorrow, to send Mary away quietly. We need to meditate on these words in order to understand the great trial that Joseph had to endure in the days preceding Jesus' birth. It was a trial similar to the sacrifice of Abraham, when God asked him for his son Isaac (cf. Gen 22): to give up what was most precious, the person most beloved.

But as in the case of Abraham, the Lord intervenes: he found the faith he was looking for and he opens up a different path, a path of love and of happiness. "Joseph," he says, "do not fear to take Mary your wife, for that which is conceived in her is of the Holy Spirit" (Mt 1:20).

The Gospel tells us about the events preceding the birth of Jesus, and the Evangelist Matthew presents them from the point of view of Saint Joseph, the betrothed of the Virgin Mary.

This Gospel passage reveals to us the greatness of Saint Joseph's heart and soul. He was following a good plan for his life, but God was reserving another plan for him, a greater mission. Joseph was a man who always listened to the voice of God, he was deeply sensitive to his secret will, he was a man attentive to the messages that came to him from the depths of his heart and from on high. He did not persist in following his own plan for his life, he did not allow bitterness to poison his soul; rather, he was ready to make himself available to the news that, in such a bewildering way, was being presented to him. By accepting himself according to God's design, Joseph fully finds himself, beyond himself. His freedom to renounce even what is his, the possession of his very life, and his full interior availability to the will of God challenge us and show us the way.

Angelus message, December 22, 2013

A Mother's Restless Love

This Monica! How many tears did that holy woman shed for her son's conversion! And today too how many mothers shed tears so that their children will return to Christ! Do not lose hope in God's grace! In the *Confessions* we read this sentence that a bishop said to Saint Monica who was asking him to help her son find the road to faith: "It is not possible that the son of so many tears should perish" (III, 12, 21). After his conversion Augustine himself, addressing God, wrote: "My mother, your faithful one, wept before you on my behalf more than mothers are wont to weep the bodily death of their children" (ibid., III, 11, 19). A restless woman, this woman who at the end of her life said these beautiful words: *"cumulatius hoc mihi Deus praestitit!"* [my God has exceeded my expectations abundantly] (ibid., IX, 10, 26). God lavishly rewarded her tearful request! And Augustine was Monica's heir, from her he received the seed of restlessness. This, then, is the restlessness of love: ceaselessly seeking the good of the other, of the beloved, without ever stopping and with the intensity that leads even to tears. . . . Do we feel the restlessness of love? . . . The restlessness of love is always an incentive to go toward the other, without waiting for the other to manifest his need.

Homily at the Basilica of Saint Augustine,
Rome, August 28, 2013

What Does a Mother Do?

I ask myself: What does a mother do? First of all, she teaches how to walk through life, she teaches the right path to take through life, she knows how to guide her children, she always tries to point out to them the right path in life for growing up and becoming adults. And she does so with tenderness, affection, and love, even when she is trying to straighten out our path because we are going a little astray in life or are taking roads that lead to an abyss. A mother knows what's important for a child to enable him to walk the right way through life. Moreover, she did not learn it from books but from her own heart. The university of mothers is their heart! They learn there how to bring up their children....

[W]hen a child grows up, becomes an adult, he chooses his path, assumes his responsibilities, stands on his own two feet, does what he likes, and at times he can also go off course; some accident occurs. A mother has the patience to continue to accompany her children, always and in every situation. It is the force of her love that impels her; a mother can follow her children on their way with discretion and tenderness and, even when they go astray, always finds a way to understand them, to be close, to help. We—in my region—say that a mother can "*dar la cara.*" What does this mean? It means that a mother can "stand up" for her children, in other words she is always motivated to defend them. I am thinking of the mothers who suffer for their children in prison or in difficult situations; they do not question whether or not their children are guilty, they keep on loving them. Mothers often suffer humiliation, but they are not afraid, they never cease to give of themselves. . . .

> " . . . a mother can follow her children on their way with discretion and tenderness and, even when they go astray. . . . "

A last thought: for her children a mother is also able to ask and knock at every door, without calculation; she does so out of love. And I think of how mothers can also and especially knock at the door of God's heart! Mothers say so many prayers for their children, especially for the weaker ones, for those in the greatest need or who have gone down dangerous or erroneous paths in life. A few weeks ago I celebrated Mass in the Church of Saint Augustine here in Rome, where the relics of Saint Monica, his mother, are preserved. How many prayers that holy mother raised to God for her son, and how many tears she shed! I am thinking of you, dear mothers: how often you pray for your children, never tiring! Continue to pray and to entrust them to God; he has a great heart! Knock at God's heart with prayers for your children.

General Audience, September 18, 2013

A Woman's Irreplaceable Role

The new opportunities and responsibilities which have opened, and which I sincerely hope may further expand by the presence and work of women, both within the ecclesial and civil and professional spheres, cannot make us forget woman's irreplaceable role in the family. The gifts of refinement, particular sensitivity, and tenderness, with which woman's spirit is richly endowed, represent not only a genuine strength for the life of the family, for spreading a climate of serenity and harmony, but a reality without which the human vocation cannot be fulfilled.

If in the world of work and in the public sphere a more incisive contribution of women's genius is important, this contribution remains essential within the family, which for us Christians is not simply a private place, but rather that "domestic Church" whose health and prosperity is a condition for the health and prosperity of the Church and of society itself. Let us think of our Lady: our Lady creates something in the Church that priests, bishops, and popes cannot create. She is the authentic feminine genius. And let us think about our Lady in families—about what our Lady does in a family. It is clear that the presence of woman in the domestic sphere is more necessary than ever, indeed for the transmission of sound moral principles and for the transmission of the faith itself to future generations.

At this point one spontaneously asks: How can one increase an effective presence in so many areas of the public sphere, in the world of work and in the places where the most important decisions are taken, and at the same time maintain a presence and preferential and wholly special attention to the family? And this is the field for discernment which, in addition to the reflection on the reality of women in society, requires assiduous and persevering prayer.

It is in dialogue with God, which is illumined by his Word and watered by the grace of the sacraments, that the Christian woman seeks ever anew to respond to the Lord's call, in her practical circumstances.

Such prayer is always supported by Mary's maternal presence. May she who cared for her divine Son, who prompted the first miracle at the wedding feast of Cana, who was present on Calvary and at Pentecost, indicate to you the path to take to deepen the meaning and role of women in society in order to be completely faithful to the Lord Jesus Christ and to your mission in the world. Thank you!

*Address to participants in a conference
sponsored by the Italian Women's Center, January 25, 2014*

Women Nurture Growth

Woman possesses this great treasure of being able to give life, of being able to bestow tenderness, of being able to bestow peace and joy. There is only one model for you: Mary, the woman of fidelity, she who did not understand what was happening but who obeyed. She who, when she learned that her cousin was in need, went to her in haste, the Virgin of Readiness. She who fled like a refugee to that foreign land to save the life of her Son. She who helped her Son to grow and stayed with him; and when her Son began to preach, she followed him. She who endured all that was happening to that little child, to that growing youth. She who stayed by her Son and told him what was the matter: "Look, they have no wine." She who, at the moment of the cross, was by him. Woman has an ability that we men do not have to give life and to bestow tenderness. You are women of the Church. Of the Church, or of the Church which is masculine? No, the Church is not a "he," the Church is a "she." The Church is feminine, like Mary. This is your place. To be Church, to form Church, to stay next to Jesus, to bestow tenderness, to journey, to nurture growth.

May Mary, Our Lady of the Caress, Our Lady of Tenderness, Our Lady of Readiness, ready to serve, point out the path to you.

Video message to Argentine young people, April 26 2014

Mothers Teach Fruitfulness

A mother helps her children grow up and wants them to grow strong; that is why she teaches them not to be lazy—which can also derive from a certain kind of wellbeing—not to sink into a comfortable lifestyle, contenting oneself with possessions. A mother takes care that her children develop better, that they grow strong, capable of accepting responsibilities, of engaging in life, of striving for great ideals. . . .

A mother then thinks of the health of her children, teaching them also *to face the difficulties of life*. You do not teach, you do not take care of health by avoiding problems, as though life were a motorway with no obstacles. A mother helps her children to see the problems of life realistically and not to get lost in them, but to confront them with courage, not to be weak, and to know how to overcome them, in a healthy balance that a mother "senses" between the area of security and the area of risk. And a mother can do this! She does not always take the child along the safe road, because in that way the child cannot develop, but neither does she leave the child only on the risky path, because that is dangerous. A mother knows how to balance things. A life without challenges does not exist, and a boy or a girl who cannot face or tackle them is a boy or girl with no backbone! . . .

"A mother helps her children to see the problems of life realistically and not to get lost in them, but to confront them with courage . . ."

Lastly, a good mother not only accompanies her children in their growth, without avoiding the problems and challenges of life; a good mother also helps them to make definitive decisions with freedom. This is not easy, but a mother knows how to do it. But what does freedom mean? It is certainly not doing whatever you want, allowing yourself to be dominated by the passions, to pass from one experience to another without discernment, to follow the fashions of the day; freedom does not mean, so to speak, throwing everything that you don't like out the window. No, that is not freedom! Freedom is given to us so that we know how to make good decisions in life! . . .

A mother teaches us how to be fruitful, to be open to life and to always bear good fruit, joyful fruit, hopeful fruit, and never to lose hope; to give life to others, physical and spiritual life.

Address of the Holy Father at the
Basilica of Saint Mary Major, May 4, 2013

Human Gratuitousness

I imagine how hectic the day of a dad or a mom is; they get up early, take their children to school, then they go to work, often in places where there are tensions and conflicts, as well as places that are far away. Before coming here, I went to the kitchen to have a coffee; the cook was there and I asked him: "How long does it take you to get home?" "About an hour and a half...." An hour and a half! And when he gets home, there are the children, his wife.... It often happens to us all that we feel alone like this. We feel weighed down by a crushing weight, and we ask ourselves: Is this life? The question stirs in our heart: What can we do so that our children, our kids, can give meaning to their lives? Because they also feel that our way of living is sometimes inhuman, and they do not know what direction to take so that life can be beautiful, and so they're happy to get up in the morning.

When I confess young married people and they tell me about their children, I always ask this question: "Do you have time to play with your children?" And so often I hear from the dad: "But, Father, when I go to work in the morning, they are sleeping, and when I come back in the evening, they are in bed sleeping." This is not life! It's a difficult cross. It's not human. When I was Archbishop in the other diocese and had more opportunities than I do today to speak with kids and young people, I realized that they are suffering from *orfandad*, that is orphanhood. Our children, your kids, are suffering like orphans! I believe that the same thing is happening in Rome. Young people are orphans with a safe road to travel, with a teacher in whom they trust, with ideals that warm the heart, with hopes that sustain the exhaustion of daily life. They are orphans, but they keep the desire for all that alive in their hearts! This is a society of orphans. Let's think about this, it's serious. Orphans, without the memory of their families: because, for example, grandparents are far away or in a retirement home; they don't have that familial presence, that familial memory. Orphans, without affection today, or with a kind of affection that is frantic: dad is tired, mom is tired, they go to bed. . . . And they are left orphans. Orphans of gratuitousness: what I was saying before, the generosity of a dad and a mom who know how to waste time just playing with their children. We need that sense of gratuitousness: in families, in parishes, and in society as a whole. And when we think of how the Lord is revealed to us through the free gift, that is, grace, it's a much more important thing. That need for human gratuitous-

> "The question stirs in our heart: What can we do so that our children, our kids, can give meaning to their lives?"

ness, which is how we open our hearts to the grace of God. Everything is free. He comes and grants us his grace. But if we don't have a sense of gratuitousness in the family, at school, in the parish, it will be very difficult for us to understand what the grace of God is, the grace that isn't sold, that isn't bought, but a present, a gift from God: it is God himself.

Address to the participants in the Roman diocesan conference on the family, June 16, 2014

The Wisdom of Parents

The Holy Spirit . . . makes the Christian "wise." Not in the sense that he has an answer for everything, that he knows everything, but in the sense that he "knows" about God, he knows how God acts, he knows when something is of God and when it is not of God; he has this wisdom which God places in our hearts.

The heart of the wise man in this sense has a taste and savor for God. And how important it is that there be Christians like this in our communities! Everything in them speaks of God and becomes a beautiful and living sign of his presence and of his love. And this is something that we cannot invent, that we cannot obtain by ourselves; it is a gift that God gives to those who make themselves docile to the Holy Spirit. We have the Holy Spirit within us, in our heart; we can listen to him, we can listen to him. If we listen to the Holy Spirit, he teaches us this way of wisdom, he endows us with wisdom, which is seeing with God's eyes, hearing with God's ears, loving with God's heart, directing things with God's judgment. This is the wisdom the Holy Spirit endows us with, and we can all have it. We only have to ask it of the Holy Spirit.

Think of a mother at home with the children; when one does something the other thinks of something else, and the poor mother goes to and fro with the problems of her children. And when mothers get tired and scold their children, is that wisdom? Scolding children —I ask you—is this wisdom? What do you say: Is it wisdom or not? No! Instead, when the mother takes her child aside and gently reproves him, saying: "Don't do this, because . . . ," and explains with great patience, is this the wisdom of God?

> "If we listen to the Holy Spirit, he teaches us this way of wisdom, he endows us with wisdom...."

Yes! It is what the Holy Spirit gives us in life! Then, in marriage for example, the two spouses—the husband and wife—argue, and then they don't look at each other, or if they do look at each other, they look at each other with displeasure: Is this the wisdom of God? No! Instead, if one says: "Ah, well, the storm has passed, let's make peace," and they begin again and go forward in peace: Is this wisdom? [The people respond: Yes!] Now, this is the gift of wisdom. May it come to our homes, may we have it with the children, may it come to us all!

General Audience, April 9, 2014

The Rights of Children

We must reaffirm the right of children to grow up in a family with a father and a mother capable of creating a suitable environment for the child's development and emotional maturity. Continuing to grow up and mature in a correct relationship represented by the masculinity and femininity of a father and a mother and thus preparing for affective maturity.

At the same time, this implies supporting the right of parents to decide the moral and religious education of their children. And in this regard I would like to express my rejection of any kind of educational experimentation on children. We cannot experiment on children and young people. They are not lab specimens! The horrors of the manipulation of education that we experienced in the great genocidal dictatorships of the twentieth century have not disappeared; they have retained a current relevance under various guises and proposals and, with the pretense of modernity, push children and young people to walk on the dictatorial path of "only one form of thought." A little over a week ago a great teacher said to me, "At times with these projects"—referring to actual educational projects—"one doesn't know whether the child is going to school or to a re-education camp."

Working for human rights presupposes the vital aim of fostering anthropological formation, of proper knowledge of the reality of the human person, and knowing how to respond to the problems and challenges posed by contemporary culture and the mentality propagated by the mass media. Obviously this does not mean we should take refuge in hidden protected areas that today are unable to foster life, that belong to a past culture. . . . No, not this; this is not good. . . . We should face the challenges the new culture launches with the positive values of the human person.

> "We should face the challenges the new culture launches with the positive values of the human person."

Address to members of the International Catholic Child Bureau, April 11, 2014

The Sanctity of Parents

I see the holiness in the patience of the People of God: a woman who is raising children, a man who works to bring home the bread, the sick, the elderly priests who have so many wounds but have a smile on their faces because they served the Lord, the sisters who work hard and live a hidden sanctity. This is for me the common sanctity. I often associate sanctity with patience: not only patience as *hypomoné* [the New Testament Greek word], taking charge of the events and circumstances of life, but also as a constancy in going forward, day by day. This is the sanctity of the militant Church also mentioned by Saint Ignatius. This was the sanctity of my parents: my dad, my mom, my grandmother Rosa who loved me so much. In my breviary I have the last will of my grandmother Rosa, and I read it often. For me it is like a prayer. She is a saint who suffered so much, also spiritually, and yet always went forward with courage.

Interview by Fr. Antonio Spadaro, SJ, August 19, 2013

Hearts Warmed
by the Word of God

I think of fathers and mothers, who are the primary educators [of their children]: how can they educate them if their consciences have not been enlightened by the Word of God? If their way of thinking and acting is not guided by the Word, what sort of example can they possibly give to their children? This is important, because then mothers and fathers complain: "Oh, this child. . . . " But you, what witness have you given the child? How have you spoken to him? Have you talked with him about the Word of God or about TV news? Fathers and mothers need to be talking about the Word of God!

And I think of catechists and of all those who are involved in education: if their hearts have not been warmed by the Word, how can they warm the hearts of others, of children, of youth, of adults? It is not enough just to read the Sacred Scriptures; we need to listen to Jesus who speaks in them: it is Jesus himself who speaks in the Scriptures, it is Jesus who speaks in them. We need to be receiving antennas that are tuned in to the Word of God in order to become broadcasting antennas! One receives and transmits. It is the Spirit of God who makes the Scriptures come alive, who makes us understand them deeply and in accord with their authentic and full meaning! Let us ask ourselves as the Synod draws near: What place does the Word of God have in my life, in my everyday life? Am I tuned in to God or to the many buzz words or to myself? This is a question that every one of us needs to ask him or herself.

> "Fathers and mothers need to be talking about the Word of God!"

Meeting with clergy and pastoral workers
in Assisi, October 4, 2013

Family Generations

"The young and the old carry history forward."

The Cornerstone
of Community

Jesus is present in the poor, he identifies with them. Saint John Chrysostom writes: "Thy Lord cometh unto thee in need . . ." (*In Matthaeum Homil.* lXVI, 3: PG 58, 629). . . . The care given to the elderly, like that of children, is an indicator of the quality of a community. When the elderly are tossed aside, when the elderly are isolated and sometimes fade away due to a lack of care, it's an awful sign! . . . A people who don't protect their elderly, who don't take care of their young, is a people without a future, a people without hope. Because the young—the children, the youth—and the old carry history forward. The children, the young, rightly have their biological strength. The elderly offer their memory. But when a community loses its memory, it's over, it's over. It's awful to see a community, a people, a culture that's lost its memory. The ninety-year-old grandma who spoke—*brava!*—she told us that there was this tendency to toss aside, this throw-away culture. To maintain a balance like this, where at the center of the world economy there are no men and women, but where money is an idol, it's necessary to throw things away. Children are thrown away, no children. Let us consider only the birth rate in Europe: in Italy, Spain, France. . . . And we throw away the elderly, behind which are attitudes of hidden euthanasia, a form of euthanasia. They aren't needed, and what isn't needed gets thrown away. . . .

> "A people who don't protect their elderly, who don't take care of their young, is a people without a future, a people without hope."

Changes in society begin with the poor and the elderly. As Jesus said: "The very stone which the builders rejected has become the head of the corner" (Mt 21:42). Likewise, the poor are in some ways this "cornerstone" for building a community. Today, unfortunately, the speculative economy makes the poor ever poorer, depriving them of the essentials, such as housing and employment. This is unacceptable! Those who live solidarity don't accept it and they take action. And this word, "solidarity"—many people want to eliminate it from the dictionary, because some cultures see it as a bad word. No! Solidarity is a Christian word!

Address to the members of the
Sant' Egidio community, June 15, 2014

The Two Poles of Life

Children and the elderly are the two poles of life and the most vulnerable as well, often the most forgotten.... Availability, the availability of a father or mother to their children, is so important: "spend time" with your children, play with your children. A society that neglects children and marginalizes the elderly severs its roots and darkens its future. And you have been assessing what our culture today is doing, haven't you? Every time a child is abandoned and an elderly person cast out, not only is it an act of injustice, but it also ensures the failure of that society. Caring for our little ones and for our elders is a choice for civilization. And also for the future, because the little ones, the children, the young people will carry society forward by their strength, their youth, and the elderly people will carry it forward by their wisdom, their memory, which they must give to us all.

And it makes me rejoice that the Pontifical Council for the Family has designed this new icon of the family, taking up the image of the Presentation of Jesus in the Temple with Mary and Joseph carrying the Child in fulfillment of the Law, and the elderly Simeon and Anna who, moved by the Holy Spirit, welcome him as the Savior. The title of the icon is meaningful: "And his mercy is from generation to generation." The Church that cares for children and the elderly becomes the mother of generations of believers and, at the same time, serves human society because a spirit of love, familiarity, and solidarity helps all people to rediscover the fatherhood and motherhood of God.

"A society that neglects children and marginalizes the elderly severs its roots and darkens its future."

Address to the Pontifical Council on the Family, October 25, 2013

Intergenerational Exchanges

Today the Church celebrates the parents of the Virgin Mary, the grandparents of Jesus, Saints Joachim and Anne. In their home, Mary came into the world, accompanied by the extraordinary mystery of the Immaculate Conception. Mary grew up in the home of Joachim and Anne; she was surrounded by their love and faith: in their home she learned to listen to the Lord and to follow his will. Saints Joachim and Anne were part of a long chain of people who had transmitted their faith and love for God, expressed in the warmth and love of family life, down to Mary, who received the Son of God in her womb and who gave him to the world, to us. How precious is the family as the privileged place for transmitting the faith! . . . How important grandparents are for family life, for passing on the human and religious heritage which is so essential for each and every society! How important it is to have intergenerational exchanges and dialogue, especially within the context of the family. The Aparecida Document says, "Children and the elderly build the future of peoples: children because they lead history forward, the elderly because they transmit the experience and wisdom of their lives" (no. 447). This relationship and this dialogue between generations is a treasure to be preserved and strengthened! In this World Youth Day, young people wish to acknowledge and honor their grandparents. They salute them with great affection. Grandparents. Let us salute grandparents. Young people salute their grandparents with great affection and they thank them for the ongoing witness of their wisdom.

"How important grandparents are for family life, for passing on the human and religious heritage which is so essential for each and every society!"

Angelus message, July 26, 2013

The Blessing of Grandparents

In a special way, old age is a time of grace, in which the Lord renews his call to us: he calls us to safeguard and transmit the faith, he calls us to pray, especially to intercede; he calls us to be close to those in need.... The elderly, grandparents, have the ability to understand the most difficult of situations: a great ability! And when they pray for these situations, their prayer is strong; it is powerful!

Grandparents, who have received the blessing to see their children's children (cf. Ps 128:6), are entrusted with a great responsibility: to transmit their life experience, their family history, the history of a community, of a people; to share wisdom with simplicity, and the faith itself—the most precious heritage! Happy is the family [with] grandparents close by! A grandfather is a father twice over and a grandmother is a mother twice over. In those countries where religious persecution has been cruel ... it was the grandparents who brought the children to be baptized in secret, to give them the faith. Well done! They were brave in persecution and they saved the faith in those countries!

But not every older person, grandfather, grandmother, has a family who can take him or her in. And so homes for the elderly are welcome . . . ; may they be real homes and not prisons! And may they be for the elderly and not for the interests of anyone else! They must not be institutions where the elderly live forgotten, hidden, and neglected. I feel close to the many elderly who live in these institutions, and I think with gratitude of those who go to visit and care for them. Homes for the elderly should be the "lungs" of humanity in a town, a neighborhood, or a parish. They should be the "sanctuaries" of humanity where one who is old and weak is cared for and protected like a big brother or sister. It is so good to go to visit an elderly person! Look at our children: sometimes we see them listless and sad; they go to visit an elderly person and become joyful!

> "Happy is the family [with] grandparents close by!"

Address to the elderly in Saint Peter's Square,
September 28, 2014

No Future without
Generational Encounter

" Honor your father and your mother, so that your days may be long in the land that the LORD your God is giving you" (Ex 20:12). A people has no future without such an encounter between generations, without children being able to accept with gratitude the witness of life from the hands of their parents. And part of this gratitude for those who gave you life is also gratitude for our heavenly Father.

There are times when generations of young people, for complex historical and cultural reasons, feel a deeper need to be independent from their parents, "breaking free," as it were, from the legacy of the older generation. It is a kind of adolescent rebellion. But unless the encounter, the meeting of generations, is reestablished, unless a new and fruitful intergenerational equilibrium is restored, what results is a serious impoverishment for everyone, and the freedom which prevails in society is actually a false freedom, which almost always becomes a form of authoritarianism.

We hear the same message in the Apostle Paul's exhortation to Timothy and, through him, to the Christian community. Jesus did not abolish the law of the family and the passing of generations, but brought it to fulfillment. The Lord formed a new family, in which bonds of kinship are less important than our relationship with him and our doing the will of God the Father. Yet the love of Jesus and the Father completes and fulfills our love of parents, brothers and sisters, and grandparents; it renews family relationships with the lymph of the Gospel and of the Holy Spirit. For this reason, Saint Paul urges Timothy, who was a pastor and hence a father to the community, to show respect for the elderly and members of families. He tells him to do so like a son: treating "older men as fathers," "older women as mothers," and "younger women as sisters" (cf. 1 Tim 5:1). The head of the community is not exempt from following the will of God in this way; indeed, the love of Christ impels him to do so with an even greater love, like the Virgin Mary, who, though she became the mother of the Messiah, felt herself driven by the love of God taking flesh within her to hasten to her elderly relative.

> "A people has no future … without children being able to accept with gratitude the witness of life from the hands of their parents."

Homily, September 28, 2014

A Fine Vintage Wine

We live in a time when the elderly don't count. It's unpleasant to say it, but they are set aside because they are considered a nuisance. [Yet] the elderly pass on history, doctrine, faith, and they leave them to us as an inheritance. They are like a fine vintage wine; that is, they have within themselves the power to give us this noble inheritance.

There was a father, mother, and their many children, and a grandfather lived with them. He was quite old, and when he was at table eating soup, he would get everything dirty: his mouth, the serviette . . . it was not a pretty sight! One day the father said that, given what was happening to the grandfather, from that day forward he would eat alone. And so [the father] bought a little table and placed it in the kitchen. And so the grandfather ate alone in the kitchen while the family ate in the dining room. After some days, the father returned home from work and found one of his children playing with wood. He asked him: "What are you doing?" to which the child replied: "I am playing carpenter." "And what are you building?" the father asked. "A table for you, Papa, for when you get old like Grandpa." This story has stayed with me for a lifetime and done me great good. Grandparents are a treasure.

> "The remembrance of our ancestors leads us to imitate their faith."

The remembrance of our ancestors leads us to imitate their faith. It is true that old age is at times unpleasant, because of the illnesses it brings. But the wisdom of our grandparents is the inheritance we ought to receive. A people that does not care for its grandparents, that does not respect its grandparents, has no future since it has lost its memory.

We would do well to think about the many elderly men and women, about those who are in rest homes and also those—it is an unpleasant word, but let us say it—who have been abandoned by their loved ones. Let us pray for them, that they may be consistent to the very end. This is the role of the elderly, this is the treasure. Let us pray for our grandfathers and grandmothers, who often played a heroic role in handing on the faith in times of persecution. Especially in times past, when fathers and mothers often were not at home or had strange ideas, confused as they were by the fashionable ideologies of the day, grandmothers were the ones who handed on the faith.

Homily, November 19, 2013

Time with Grandparents

Young people coming together with their grandparents is key. Several bishops from countries in a state of crisis, where the unemployment rate among young people is high, were telling me part of the solution for young people lies in the fact that their grandparents are supporting them. They re-encounter their grandparents, who have a pension, and so leave their retirement homes and return to the family; what is more, they bring back with them their memory, that encounter.

I remember a film I saw some twenty-five years ago, by the famous Japanese director, Kurosawa. It was very simple: a family—two children, a father, and a mother. The father and mother travel to the United States, leaving the children with their grandmother. Japanese children, Coca Cola, hot dogs . . . this sort of culture. And the film tells the story of how these children, little by little, begin to listen to what their grandmother tells them about the historical memory of their people. When the parents return, it is the parents who are disoriented: they are far from that memory the children received from their grandmother.

This phenomenon of children and young people spending time with their grandparents preserved the faith in the countries of the East during the Communist era, because the parents were not able to go to Church. In recent days, some were telling me—perhaps I am getting confused . . . I don't know who, the Bulgarian Bishops or those from Albania—they were telling me that their churches are filled with the elderly and with young people: the parents don't go, because they have never encountered Jesus. This in parentheses . . . children and young people spending time with their grandparents is crucial for receiving the memory of their people and for discerning the present: to become teachers of discernment, spiritual advisors. And here, we see its importance with regard to transmitting the faith to young people, a "one-on-one" apostolate.

> " … children and young people spending time with their grandparents is crucial for receiving the memory of their people and for discerning the present…"

Address to the Pontifical Commission of Latin America, February 28, 2014

Three Paths for Young People

S ports are a means for education. I find there are three paths for young people, for children and little ones. The path of education, the path of sports, and the path of work, when there are jobs for young people to start with! If there [were] these three paths, I assure you there wouldn't be dependencies: no drugs, no alcohol! Why? Because school leads you forward, sports lead you forward, and work leads you forward. Don't forget this. . . .

It is important, dear boys and girls, that sports remain a game! Only by remaining a game will it do good for the body and spirit. And as sportsmen, I invite you not only to play, like you already do, but there is something more: challenge yourself in the game of life like you are in the game of sports. Challenge yourself in the quest for good, in both Church and society, without fear, with courage and enthusiasm. Get involved with others and with God. Don't settle for a mediocre "tie"; give it your best, spend your life on what really matters and lasts forever. Don't settle for lukewarm lives, "mediocre, even-scored" lives: no, no! Go forward, seek victory, always!

In sports clubs one learns how to accept. One accepts every athlete who wishes to join; they accept one another with simplicity and kindness. I invite all managers and coaches to be, above all, accepting people, capable of holding the door open to give each one, especially the least fortunate, an opportunity to express himself.

And you, boys and girls, who experience joy when you receive your jerseys, the sign of belonging to your team, you are called to behave like true athletes, worthy of the jerseys you wear. I hope you can merit them every day through your commitment as well as your hard work.

I also hope you can taste the beauty of teamwork, which is so important in life. No individualism! "No" to playing for yourselves. In my homeland, when a player does this, we say: "This guy wants to devour the ball all by himself!" No, this is individualism: don't devour the ball; be team players. To belong to a sports club means to reject every form of selfishness and isolation, it is an opportunity to encounter and be with others, to help one another, to compete in mutual esteem and to grow in brotherhood.

. . . I recommend that everyone get to play, not just the best, but everyone, with the advantages and the limitations that each has, indeed, focusing on the disadvantaged, as Jesus did. And I encourage you to carry on with your commitment through sports for children from the outskirts of cities; in addition to footballs, you can give them reasons for hope and trust. Always remember these three paths: school, sports, and job opportunities. Seek this always. And I assure [you] that this road won't lead to drug or alcohol dependencies and other vices.

Address to Sports Associations, June 7, 2014

Children Need to Be Accepted and Protected

The Child Jesus, born in Bethlehem, is the sign given by God to those who awaited salvation, and he remains forever the sign of God's tenderness and presence in our world. The angel announces to the shepherds: "This will be a sign for you: you will find a child. . . . "

Today, too, children are a sign. They are a sign of hope, a sign of life, but also a "diagnostic" sign, a marker indicating the health of families, society, and the entire world. Wherever children are accepted, loved, cared for, and protected, the family is healthy, society is more healthy, and the world is more human.

To us, the men and women of the twenty-first century, God today also says: "This will be a sign for you"; look to the child. . . .

The Child of Bethlehem is frail, like all newborn children. He cannot speak and yet he is the Word made flesh, who came to transform the hearts and lives of all men and women. This Child, like every other child, is vulnerable; he needs to be accepted and protected. Today, too, children need to be welcomed and defended from the moment of their conception.

Sadly, in this world, with all its highly developed technology, great numbers of children continue to live in inhuman situations, on the fringes of society, in the peripheries of great cities and in the countryside. All too many children continue to be exploited, maltreated, enslaved, prey to violence and illicit trafficking. Still too many children live in exile, as refugees, at times lost at sea, particularly in the waters of the Mediterranean. Today, in acknowledging this, we feel shame before God, before God who became a child.

And we have to ask ourselves: Who are we, as we stand before the Child Jesus? Who are we, as we stand before today's children? Are we like Mary and Joseph, who welcomed Jesus and cared for him with the love of a father and a mother? Are we ready to be there for children, to "waste time" with them? Are we ready to listen to them, to care for them, to pray for them and with them? Or do we ignore them because we are too caught up in our own affairs?

> "Wherever children are accepted, loved, cared for, and protected, the family is healthy, society is more healthy and the world is more human."

Homily, May 25, 2014

In Difficult Times

"Dear families, the Lord knows our struggles: he knows them."

The Gift of Counsel

A s with all of the other gifts of the Spirit . . . counsel too constitutes a treasure for the whole Christian community. The
Lord does not only speak to us in the intimacy of the heart; yes, he
speaks to us, but not only there; he also speaks to us through the
voice and witness of the brethren. It is truly a great gift to be able
to meet men and women of faith who, especially in the most complicated and important stages of our lives, help us to bring light to
our heart and to recognize the Lord's will!

I remember once at the Shrine of Luján I was in the confes-
sional, where there was a long queue. There was even a very mod-
ern young man, with earrings, tattoos, all these things. . . . And he
came to tell me what was happening to him. It was a big and difficult problem. And he said to me: "I told my mother all this and
my mother said to me, 'Go to our Lady and she will tell you what
you must do.'" Here is a woman who had the gift of counsel. She
did not know how to help her son out of his problem, but she
indicated the right road: go to our Lady and she will tell you. This

is the gift of counsel. That humble, simple woman gave her son the truest counsel. In fact, this young man said to me: "I looked at our Lady and I felt that I had to do this, this and this. . . . " I did not have to speak, his mother and the boy himself had already said everything. This is the gift of counsel. You mothers who have this gift, ask it for your children; the gift of giving good counsel to your children is a gift of God.

"It is truly a great gift to be able to meet men and women of faith who, especially in the most complicated and important stages of our lives, help us to bring light to our heart and to recognize the Lord's will!"

Dear friends, Psalm 16 [15] . . . invites us to pray with these words: "I bless the LORD who gives me counsel; in the night also my heart instructs me. I keep the LORD always before me; because he is at my right hand, I shall not be moved" (vv. 7–8). May the Spirit always pour this certainty into our heart and fill us thus with the consolation of his peace! Always ask for the gift of counsel.

General Audience, May 7, 2014

God Is Present

The Gospel presents the Holy Family to us on the sorrowful road of exile, seeking refuge in Egypt. Joseph, Mary, and Jesus experienced the tragic fate of refugees, which is marked by fear, uncertainty, and unease (cf. Mt 2:13–15; 19–23). Unfortunately, in our own time, millions of families can identify with this sad reality. Almost every day the television and papers carry news of refugees fleeing from hunger, war, and other grave dangers, in search of security and a dignified life for themselves and for their families.

In distant lands, even when they find work, refugees and immigrants do not always find a true welcome, respect, and appreciation for the values they bring. Their legitimate expectations collide with complex and difficult situations which at times seem insurmountable. Therefore, as we fix our gaze on the Holy Family of Nazareth as they were forced to become refugees, let us think of the tragedy of those migrants and refugees who are victims of rejection and exploitation, who are victims of human trafficking and of slave labor. But let us also think of the other "exiles": I would call them "hidden exiles," those exiles who can be found within their own families: the elderly, for example, who are sometimes treated as a burdensome presence. I often think that a good indicator for knowing how a family is doing is seeing how their children and elderly are treated.

> "Jesus wanted to belong to a family which experienced these hardships, so that no one would feel excluded from the loving closeness of God."

Jesus wanted to belong to a family which experienced these hardships, so that no one would feel excluded from the loving closeness of God. The flight into Egypt caused by Herod's threat shows us that God is present where man is in danger, where man is suffering, where he is fleeing, where he experiences rejection and abandonment; but God is also present where man dreams, where he hopes to return in freedom to his homeland and plans and chooses life for his family and dignity for himself and his loved ones.

Angelus message, December 29, 2013

Praying in the
Battle Against Evil

I n [the] Gospel Jesus tells a parable on the need to pray always, never wearying. The main character is a widow whose insistent pleading with a dishonest judge succeeds in obtaining justice from him. Jesus concludes: if the widow succeeded in convincing that judge, do you think that God will not listen to us if we pray to him with insistence? Jesus' words are very strong: "And will not God vindicate his elect, who cry to him day and night?" (Lk 18:7)

"Crying day and night" to God! This image of prayer is striking, but let us ask ourselves: Why does God want this? Doesn't he already know what we need? What does it mean to "insist" with God?

This is a good question that makes us examine an important aspect of the faith: God invites us to pray insistently not because he is unaware of our needs or because he is not listening to us. On the contrary, he is always listening and he knows everything about us lovingly. On our daily journey, especially in times of difficulty, in the battle against the evil that is outside and within us, the Lord is not far away, he is by our side. We battle with him beside us, and our weapon is prayer which makes us feel his presence beside us, his mercy, and also his help. But the battle against evil is a long and hard one; it requires patience and endurance, like Moses who had to keep his arms outstretched for the people to prevail (cf. Ex 17:8–13). This is how it is: there is a battle to be waged each day, but God is our ally, faith in him is our strength and prayer is the expression of this faith. Therefore Jesus assures us of the victory, but at the end he asks: "when the Son of man comes, will he find faith on earth?" (Lk 18:8). If faith is snuffed out, prayer is snuffed out, and we walk in the dark. We become lost on the path of life.

> "On our daily journey, especially in times of difficulty, in the battle against the evil that is outside and within us, the Lord is not far away, he is by our side."

Therefore, let us learn from the widow of the Gospel to pray always without growing weary. This widow was very good! She knew how to battle for her children! I think of the many women who fight for their families, who pray and never grow weary. Today let us all remember these women who by their attitude provide us with a true witness of faith and courage and a model of prayer. Our thoughts go out to them!

Angelus message, October 20, 2013

Persevering in Love

Jesus never tires of loving his Church. It is a fruitful love. It is a faithful love. Jesus is the faithful one. Saint Paul, in one of his letters, says that if you confess Christ, he will confess you before the Father; if you deny Christ, he will deny you; even if you are not faithful to Christ, he remains faithful, for he cannot deny himself! Fidelity is the essence of Jesus' love. Jesus' love in his Church is faithful. This faithfulness is like a light on marriage. The fidelity of love. Always.

. . . Married life must be persevering, because otherwise love cannot go forward. Perseverance in love, in good times and in difficult times, when there are problems: problems with children, economic problems, problems here, problems there—but love perseveres, presses on, always trying to work things out, to save the family. Persevering: they get up every morning, the man and the woman, and carry the family forward. . . .

These marriages, in which the spouses do not want children, in which the spouses want to remain without fertility. This culture of well-being from ten years ago convinced us: "It's better not to have children! It's better! You can go explore the world, go on holiday; you can have a villa in the countryside; you can be carefree. . . . It might be better—more comfortable—to have a dog, two cats, and the love goes to the two cats and the dog." Is this true or is this not? Have you seen it? Then, in the end, this marriage comes to old age in solitude, with the bitterness of loneliness. It is not fruitful, it does not do what Jesus does with his Church: He makes his Church fruitful.

> " . . . love perseveres, presses on, always trying to work things out, to save the family."

Homily, June 2, 2014

Marital Healing in
the Cross of Christ

Today's first reading [Num 21:4–9] speaks to us of the people's journey through the desert. We can imagine them as they walked, led by Moses; they were families: fathers, mothers, sons and daughters, grandparents, men and women of all ages, accompanied by many children and the elderly who struggled to make the journey. This people reminds us of the Church as she makes her way across the desert of the contemporary world, reminds us of the People of God composed, for the most part, of families.

. . . At a certain point, "the people became impatient on the way" (Num 21:4). They are tired, water supplies are low, and all they have for food is manna, which, although plentiful and sent by God, seems far too meager in a time of crisis. And so they complain and protest against God and against Moses: "Why did you make us leave? . . . " (cf. Num 21:5). They are tempted to turn back and abandon the journey.

Here our thoughts turn to married couples who "become impatient on the way," the way of conjugal and family life. The hardship of the journey causes them to experience interior weariness; they lose the flavor of matrimony and they cease to draw water from the well of the sacrament. Daily life becomes burdensome and, often, even "nauseating."

> "Whoever entrusts himself to Jesus crucified receives the mercy of God and finds healing from the deadly poison of sin."

During such moments of disorientation—the Bible says—poisonous serpents come and bite the people, and many die. This causes the people to repent and to turn to Moses for forgiveness, asking him to beseech the Lord so that he will cast out the snakes. Moses prays to the Lord, and the Lord offers a remedy: a bronze serpent set on a pole; whoever looks at it will be saved from the deadly poison of the vipers.

What is the meaning of this symbol? God does not destroy the serpents, but, rather, offers an "antidote": by means of the bronze serpent fashioned by Moses, God transmits his healing strength, namely his mercy, which is more potent than the Tempter's poison.

As we have heard in the Gospel, Jesus identifies himself with this symbol: out of love the Father "has given" his only begotten Son so that men and women might have eternal life (cf. Jn 3:13–17). Such immense love of the Father spurs the Son to become man, to become a servant and to die for us upon a cross.... Whoever entrusts himself to Jesus crucified receives the mercy of God and finds healing from the deadly poison of sin.

The cure which God offers the people applies also, in a particular way, to spouses who "have become impatient on the way" and who succumb to the dangerous temptation of discouragement, infidelity, weakness, abandonment. . . . To them, too, God the Father gives his Son Jesus, not to condemn them, but to save them; if they entrust themselves to him, he will bring them healing by the merciful love which pours forth from the cross, with the strength of his grace that renews and sets married couples and families once again on the right path.

Homily, September 14, 2014

The Lord Knows Our Struggles

I have felt the pain of families living in situations of poverty and war. I have listened to young people who want to be married even though they face numerous difficulties. . . . Let us ask ourselves: How is it possible to live the joy which comes from faith, in the family, today? But I ask you also: Is it possible to live this joy or is it not possible?

A saying of Jesus in the Gospel of Matthew speaks to us: *"Come to me, all who labor and are heavy laden, and I will give you rest"* (Mt 11:28). Life is often wearisome, and many times tragically so. . . . Work is tiring; looking for work is exhausting. And finding work today requires much effort. But what is most burdensome in life is not this. What weighs more than all of these things is a lack of love. It weighs upon us never to receive a smile, not to be welcomed. Certain silences are oppressive, even at times within families, between husbands and wives, between parents and children, among siblings. Without love, the burden becomes even heavier, intolerable. I think of elderly people living alone, and families who receive no help in caring for someone at home with special needs. "Come to me, all who labor and are heavy laden," Jesus says.

Dear families, the Lord knows our struggles; he knows them. He knows the burdens we have in our lives. But the Lord also knows our great desire to find joy and rest! Do you remember? Jesus said, " . . . that your joy may be complete" (cf. Jn 15:11). Jesus wants our joy to be complete! He said this to the apostles and today he says it to us. Here, then, is the first thing I would like to share with you this evening, and it is a saying of Jesus: Come to me, families from around the world—Jesus says—and I will give you rest, so that your joy may be complete. Take home this word of Jesus, carry it in your hearts, share it with the family. It invites us to come to Jesus so that he may give this joy to us and to everyone.

> "Come to me, families from around the world—Jesus says—and I will give you rest, so that your joy may be complete."

Address to the Pilgrimage of Families, October 26, 2013

Daily Martyrdom

What does it mean "to lose one's life for the sake of Jesus"? This can happen in two ways: explicitly by confessing the faith, or implicitly by defending the truth. Martyrs are the greatest example of losing one's life for Christ. In 2,000 years, a vast host of men and women have sacrificed their lives to remain faithful to Jesus Christ and his Gospel. And today, in many parts of the world, there are many, many—more than in the first centuries—so many martyrs, who give up their lives for Christ, who are brought to death because they do not deny Jesus Christ. This is our Church. Today we have more martyrs than in the first centuries! However, there is also daily martyrdom, which may not entail death but is still a "loss of life" for Christ, by doing one's duty with love, according to the logic of Jesus, the logic of gift, of sacrifice. Let us think: How many dads and moms every day put their faith into practice by offering up their own lives in a concrete way for the good of the family! Think about this! How many priests, brothers, and sisters carry out their service generously for the Kingdom of God! How many young people renounce their own interests in order to dedicate themselves to children, the disabled, the elderly. . . . They are martyrs too! Daily martyrs, martyrs of everyday life!

" ... how many dads and moms every day put their faith into practice by offering up their own lives in a concrete way for the good of the family!"

. . . How many people pay dearly for their commitment to truth! Upright people who are not afraid to go against the current! How many just men prefer to go against the current, so as not to deny the voice of conscience, the voice of truth!

And we, we must not be afraid! Among you are many young people. To you young people I say: Do not be afraid to go against the current, when they want to rob us of hope, when they propose rotten values, values like food gone bad—and when food has gone bad, it harms us; these values harm us. We must go against the current! And you young people are the first: Go against the tide and have the daring to move precisely against the current. Forward, be brave and go against the tide! And be proud of doing so.

Angelus message, June 23, 2013

A Prayer for the Unemployed

I want . . . to express my closeness to you, especially to the situations of suffering: to the many young people out of work, to people on unemployment benefits, or [employed] on a temporary basis, to business and trades people who find it hard to keep going. I am very familiar with this situation because of my experience in Argentina. I myself was spared it but my family wasn't. My father went to Argentina as a young man full of illusions "of making it in America." And he suffered in the dreadful recession of the 1930s. They lost everything! There was no work! And in my childhood I heard talk of this period at home. . . . I never saw it, I had not yet been born, but I heard about this suffering at home, I heard talk of it. I know it well! However, I must say to you: "Courage!" Nevertheless I am also aware that for my own part I must do everything to ensure that this term "courage" is not a beautiful word spoken in passing! May it not be merely the smile of a courteous employee, a Church employee who comes and says, "Be brave!" No! I don't want this! I want courage to come from within me and to impel me to do everything as a pastor, as a man. We must all face this challenge with solidarity, among you—also among us—we must all face with solidarity and intelligence this historic struggle.

> "Perhaps hope is like embers under the ashes; let us help each other with solidarity, blowing on the ashes to rekindle the flame."

. . . I have written a few things down for you, but on seeing you these words came to me. I shall give the bishop this written text as if they had been spoken; but I preferred to tell you what welled up from my heart as I look at you now! You know, it is easy to say don't lose hope. But to . . . you all, those who have work and those who don't, I say, "Do not let yourself be robbed of hope! Do not let yourselves be robbed of hope!" Perhaps hope is like embers under the ashes; let us help each other with solidarity, blowing on the ashes to rekindle the flame. But hope carries us onward. That is not optimism, it is something else. However, hope does not belong to any one person; we all create hope! We must sustain hope in everyone, among all of you and among all of us who are far away. Hope is both yours and ours. It is something that belongs to everyone! This is why I am saying to you: "Do not let yourselves be robbed of hope!" But let us be cunning, for the Lord tells us that idols are more clever than we are. The Lord asks us to have the wisdom of serpents and the innocence of doves. Let us acquire this cunning and call things by their proper name. At this time, in our economic system, in our proposed globalized system of life there is an idol [i.e., money] at the center, and this is unacceptable! Let us all fight so that there may be men and

women, families, all of us at the center—at least of our own life—
so that hope can make headway. . . . "Do not let yourselves be
robbed of hope!"

I would now like to finish by praying with you all in
silence. . . . I shall say to you whatever wells up in my heart and
please pray with me in silence.

> Lord God, look down upon us! Look at this city, this
> island. Look upon our families.

> Lord, you were not without a job, you were a carpenter,
> you were happy.

> Lord, we have no work.

> The idols want to rob us of our dignity. The unjust systems
> want to rob us of hope.

> Lord, do not leave us on our own. Help us to help each
> other; so that we forget our selfishness a little and feel
> in our heart the "we," the we of a people who want to
> keep on going.

> Lord Jesus, you were never out of work; give us work and
> teach us to fight for work and bless us all. In the name
> of the Father, of the Son, and of the Holy Spirit.

Meeting with workers, September 22, 2013

The Gift of Fortitude

There are . . . difficult moments and extreme situations in which the gift of fortitude manifests itself in an extraordinary, exemplary way. This is the case with those who are facing particularly harsh and painful situations that disrupt their lives and those of their loved ones. The Church shines with the testimony of so many brothers and sisters who have not hesitated to give their very lives in order to remain faithful to the Lord and his Gospel. Even today there is no shortage of Christians who in many parts of the world continue to celebrate and bear witness to their faith with deep conviction and serenity, and persist even when they know that this may involve them paying a higher price. We too, all of us, know people who have experienced difficult situations and great suffering. Let us think of those men, of those women who have a difficult life, who fight to feed their family, to educate their children; they do all of this because the spirit of fortitude is helping them. How many men and women there are—we do not know their names—who honor our people, who honor our Church, because they are strong: strong in carrying forward their lives, their family, their work, their faith. These brothers and sisters of ours are saints, everyday saints, hidden saints among us; the gift of fortitude is what enables them to carry on with their duties as individuals, fathers, mothers, brothers, sisters, citizens. We have many of them! Let us thank the Lord for these Christians who live in hidden holiness: the Holy Spirit is within them, carrying them forward! And it will benefit us to think about these people: if they do all of this, if they can do it, why can't I? And it will also do us good to ask the Lord to give us the gift of fortitude.

We need not think that the gift of fortitude is necessary only on some occasions or in particular situations. This gift must constitute the tenor of our Christian life, in the ordinary daily routine. As I said, we need to be strong every day of our lives, to carry forward our life, our family, our faith. The Apostle Paul said something that will benefit us to hear: "I can do all things in him who strengthens me" (Phil 4:13). When we face daily life, when difficulties arise, let us remember this: "I can do all things in him who strengthens me." The Lord always strengthens us, he never lets strength lack. The Lord does not try us beyond our possibilities. He is always with us. "I can do all things in him who strengthens me."

Dear friends, sometimes we may be tempted to give in to laziness, or, worse, to discouragement, especially when faced with the hardships and trials of life. In these cases, let us not lose heart; let us invoke the Holy Spirit so that through the gift of fortitude he may lift our heart and communicate new strength and enthusiasm to our life and to our following of Jesus.

Audience, May 14, 2014

God Can Untangle the Knots

When children disobey their parents, we can say that a little "knot" is created. This happens if the child acts with an awareness of what he or she is doing, especially if there is a lie involved. At that moment, they break trust with their parents. You know how frequently this happens! Then the relationship with their parents needs to be purified of this fault; the child has to ask forgiveness so that harmony and trust can be restored. Something of the same sort happens in our relationship with God. When we do not listen to him, when we do not follow his will, we do concrete things that demonstrate our lack of trust in him—for that is what sin is—and a kind of knot is created deep within us. These knots take away our peace and serenity. They are dangerous, since many knots can form a tangle which gets more and more painful and difficult to undo.

But we know one thing: nothing is impossible for God's mercy! Even the most tangled knots are loosened by his grace. And Mary, whose "yes" opened the door for God to undo the knot of the ancient disobedience, is the Mother who patiently and lovingly brings us to God, so that he can untangle the knots of our soul by his fatherly mercy. We all have some of these knots and we can ask in our heart of hearts: What are the knots in my life? "Father, my knots cannot be undone!" It is a mistake to say anything of the sort! All the knots of our heart, every knot of our conscience, can be undone. Do I ask Mary to help me trust in God's mercy, to undo those knots, to change? She, as a woman of faith, will surely tell you: "Get up, go to the Lord: he understands you." And she leads us by the hand as a Mother, our Mother, to the embrace of our Father, the Father of mercies.

> "But we know one thing: nothing is impossible for God's mercy! Even the most tangled knots are loosened by his grace."

Address during the Marian prayer vigil
for the Year of Faith, October 12, 2013

Families in the World

*"How many attacks there are against the basic values
that constitute the fabric of family life
and of social coexistence!"*

Economics Must Serve Humanity

The goal of economics and politics is to serve humanity, beginning with the poorest and most vulnerable wherever they may be, even in their mothers' wombs. Every economic and political theory or action must set about providing each inhabitant of the planet with the minimum wherewithal to live in dignity and freedom, with the possibility of supporting a family, educating children, praising God, and developing one's own human potential. This is the main thing; in the absence of such a vision, all economic activity is meaningless.

In this sense, the various grave economic and political challenges facing today's world require a courageous change of attitude that will restore to the end (the human person) and to the means (economics and politics) their proper place. Money and other political and economic means must serve, not rule, bearing in mind that, in a seemingly paradoxical way, free and disinterested solidarity is the key to the smooth functioning of the global economy.

I wished to share these thoughts . . . with a view to highlighting what is implicit in all political choices, but can sometimes be forgotten: the primary importance of putting humanity, every single man and woman, at the center of all political and economic activity, both nationally and internationally, because man is the truest and deepest resource for politics and economics, as well as their ultimate end.

Letter to the British Prime Minister
on the occasion of the G8 Meeting, June 15, 2013

It Takes a Village

Teachers are the first ones who must remain open to reality . . . with minds still open to learning! For if a teacher is not open to learning, he or she is not a good teacher and isn't even interesting; young people understand that, they have a "nose" for it, and they are attracted by professors whose thoughts are open, "unfinished," who are seeking something "more," and thus they infect students with this attitude. This is one of the reasons why I love school.

Another reason is that school is a place of encounter. For we are all on a journey, beginning a process, on our way down a road. And . . . school . . . is not a parking lot. It is a meeting place along the way. We meet our peers; we meet teachers; we meet the staff. Parents meet the professors; the principal meets the families, etc. It is a place of encounter. And we need this culture of encounter today in order to get to know one another, to love one another, to journey together. And this is fundamental precisely in the years of growth and development, as a complement to the family. The family is the first core for relationships: the relationship with one's father and mother and with one's brothers and sisters is the basis, and it always accompanies us in life. But at school we "socialize": we meet people who are different from us, different in age, culture, roots, abilities. School is the first society that integrates the family. Family and school should never be opposed! They are complementary, and therefore it is important that they cooperate in mutual respect. And families of the children in one class can do a great deal by jointly cooperating among themselves and with the teachers. This makes me think of a very nice African proverb which goes: "It takes a village to raise a child." It takes many people to educate and form a young person: family, teachers, staff, professors, everyone! Do you like this African proverb? So you like it? Let us say it together: It takes a village to raise a child! Together! It takes a village to raise a child! Think about this.

> "School is the first society that integrates the family. Family and school should never be opposed!"

Address to students and teachers, May 10, 2014

A "Throw-Away" Culture

We know that human life is sacred and inviolable. Every civil right rests on the recognition of the first and fundamental right, that of life, which is not subordinate to any condition, be it quantitative, economic, or, least of all, ideological. "Just as the commandment 'Thou shalt not kill' sets a clear limit in order to safeguard the value of human life, today we also have to say 'thou shalt not' to an economy of exclusion and inequality. Such an economy kills. . . . Human beings are themselves considered consumer goods to be used and then discarded. We have created a 'throw-away' culture which is now spreading" (Apostolic Exhortation *Evangelii Gaudium*, no. 53). And in this way life too ends up being thrown away.

One of the gravest risks our epoch faces, amid the opportunities offered by a market equipped with every technological innovation, is the divorce between economics and morality; the basic ethical norms of human nature are increasingly neglected. It is therefore necessary to express the strongest possible opposition to every direct attack on life, especially against the innocent and defenseless, and the unborn in a mother's womb is the example of innocence par excellence. Let us remember the words of the Second Vatican Council: "Life must be protected with the utmost care from the moment of conception: abortion and infanticide are abominable crimes" (Pastoral Constitution *Gaudium et Spes*, no. 51). I remember once, a long time ago, I had a conference with medical doctors. After the conference I greeted the doctors—this happened a long, long time ago. I was greeting the doctors, speaking to them, and one called me aside. He was holding a parcel and said to me: "Father, I want to leave this with you. These are the instruments that I used to perform abortions. I have met the Lord, I have repented and now I fight for life." He handed me all these instruments. Pray for this good man!

> "One of the gravest risks our epoch faces, amid the opportunities offered by a market equipped with every technological innovation, is the divorce between economics and morality…"

Anyone who is Christian has a duty to bear witness to the Gospel: to protect life courageously and lovingly in all its phases. I encourage you to do this always with closeness, proximity, so that every woman may feel respected as a person, heard, accepted, and supported.

Address to Italian Pro-life Movement, April 11, 2014

Life: Precious in Old Age
and Disability

"We have created a 'throw-away' culture, which is now spreading. It is no longer simply about exploitation and oppression, but something new. Exclusion ultimately has to do with what it means to be a part of the society in which we live; those excluded are no longer society's underside or its fringes or its disenfranchised—they are no longer even a part of it. The excluded are not the 'exploited' but the outcast, the 'leftovers'" (*Evangelii Gaudium*, no. 53). The socio-demographic situation of the aged clearly reveals to us this exclusion of the elderly, especially when he or she is ill, disabled, or vulnerable for any reason. One too often forgets, in fact, that human relationships are always relationships of mutual dependence, which is manifest to different degrees over the course of a person's life and which becomes most apparent in old age, illness, disability, and suffering in general. And this requires that, in interpersonal relationships such as those which exist in a community, we offer the necessary help, in order to seek to respond to the need the person presents at that moment. However, at the basis of discrimination and exclusion there lies an anthropological question: What is man's worth and what is the basis of his worth? Health is certainly an important value, but it does not determine the value of a person. Furthermore, health in and of itself is no guarantee of happiness—for this may occur even in the presence of poor health. The fullness toward which every human life tends is not in contradiction with a condition of illness and suffering. Therefore, poor health and disability are never a good reason for excluding or, worse, for eliminating a person; and the most serious privation that elderly persons undergo is not the weakening of the body and the disability that may ensue, but abandonment and exclusion, the privation of love.

> "A society truly welcomes life when it recognizes that it is also precious in old age, in disability, in serious illness and even when it is fading…"

The family, instead, is the teacher of acceptance and solidarity; it is within the family that education substantially draws upon relationships of solidarity; in the family one learns that the loss of health is not a reason for discriminating against human life; the family teaches us not to fall into individualism and to balance the "I" with the "we."

It is there that "taking care of one another" becomes a foundation of human life and a moral attitude to foster, through the values of commitment and solidarity. The witness of the family is crucial, before the whole of society, in reaffirming the importance of an elderly person as a member of a community, who has his or her own mission to accomplish and who only seemingly receives with nothing to offer. . . .

A society truly welcomes life when it recognizes that it is also precious in old age, in disability, in serious illness, and even when it is fading; when it teaches that the call to human fulfillment does not exclude suffering; indeed, when it teaches its members to see in the sick and suffering a gift for the entire community, a presence that summons them to solidarity and responsibility. This is the Gospel of life which . . . sustained by grace, you are called to spread.

Message to the General Assembly of the
Pontifical Academy for Life, February 19, 2014

Using People
as Disposable Goods

It is impossible to remain indifferent knowing that there are human beings who are treated like merchandise! Think of the children adopted for organ transplants, of women who are deceived and forced into prostitution, of exploited workers without rights or a voice, etc. This is human trafficking! "It is precisely on this level that we need to make a good examination of conscience: How many times have we permitted a human being to be seen as an object, to be put on show in order to sell a product or to satisfy an immoral desire? The human person ought never to be sold or bought as if he or she were a commodity. Whoever uses human persons in this way and exploits them, even if indirectly, becomes an accomplice of this injustice" (Address to the new Ambassadors, December 12, 2013). If we then go to the family level and enter a home, how often does abuse reign! Parents who enslave their children, children who enslave their parents; spouses who forget their promises, who use each other as if they were disposable goods, goods to be used and thrown away; elderly without a place, and children and adolescents with no voice. How many attacks there are against the basic values that constitute the fabric of family life and of social coexistence! Yes, there is the need for a deep examination of conscience. How can we proclaim the joy of Easter without supporting those who are deprived of their freedom on this earth?

Message for Lenten Brotherhood Campaign
in Brazil, February 25, 2014

The Tools of Creativity
and Solidarity

Man's dignity is tied to work. I listened to several young workers who are unemployed, and this is what they told me: "Father, we at home—my wife, my children—we eat every day because they give us something to eat at the parish, or the club, or the Red Cross. But Father, I don't know what it means to earn bread for the table, and I need to eat, but I need to know the dignity of being a breadwinner." And work means this! This dignity is wounded where work is lacking! Anyone who is unemployed or underemployed is likely, in fact, to be placed on the margins of society, becoming a victim of social exclusion. Many times it happens that people without work—I am thinking especially of the many unemployed young people today—slip into chronic discouragement, or worse, into apathy.

. . . Work is a good for everyone and it needs to be available for everyone. Periods of grave hardship and unemployment need to be addressed with the tools of creativity and solidarity. The creativity of entrepreneurs and brave artisans who look to the future with confidence and hope. And solidarity requires that all members of society renounce something and adopt a more sober lifestyle to help all those who are in need.

> "A faith received with joy and lived fully and generously can confer a humanizing force on society."

This great challenge calls the entire Christian community to action. . . . Here is the guiding principle of the choices made by a Christian: his faith. Faith moves mountains! The Christian faith can enrich society through the concrete fraternity that it bears within itself. A faith received with joy and lived fully and generously can confer a humanizing force on society. For this reason, we are all called to seek new ways to bear courageous witness to a living and life-giving faith.

Dear brothers and sisters, never stop hoping for a better future. Fight for it, fight. Do not be trapped in the vortex of pessimism, please! If each one does his or her part, if everyone always places the human person—not money—with his dignity at the center, if an attitude of solidarity and fraternal sharing inspired by the Gospel is strengthened, you will be able to leave behind the morass of a hard and difficult economic season of work.

Address to managers and workers
of the Terni Steel Mill, March 20, 2014

Where Does Our Future Lie?

Nowadays, through the economy that has taken root in the world, which has at its center the god of money and not the human person, everything is ordered to this center and whatever does not fit according to this logic is discarded. "Left-over" babies, babies who are bothersome or whose arrival is inconvenient, are simply thrown away.... The old, too, are discarded ... and in some countries of Latin America there is hidden euthanasia, hidden euthanasia! Because social services pay only up to a certain point, and no more, so the poor old people make do as they can. I remember visiting a retirement home for the elderly in Buenos Aires, which belonged to the State. The beds were all occupied; so they were putting mattresses on the floor, and the elderly just lay there. A country cannot buy a bed? This is indicative of something else, is it not? They are like waste material. Soiled sheets, with every sort of filth; without a napkin, and the poor old people were eating there, they were wiping their mouths with the sheet.... I saw this with my own eyes, no one told me about it. They are treated like trash; and this worries us . . . here I return to the issue of the young.

Today, the number of young people in need of work are a great burden on this global system; the unemployment rates among young people are so high. We have a generation of young people who have not yet experienced their own dignity. It isn't that they don't have anything to eat, because their grandparents feed them, or the parish, or state-run social assistance, or the Salvation Army, or their local club. . . . They have bread to eat, but not the dignity of having earned their bread to take home! Today young people have become part of this gamut of waste material.

And so, in the throw-away culture, we find young people who need us more than ever; not only to help them with their dreams—because in a young person without work the sense of utopia is anaesthetized, or he is on the verge of losing it altogether . . . drugs are spreading among these young people. It is not just a problem of vice, there are many forms of addiction. As in all times of epic change, strange phenomena exist such as the proliferation of dependencies: compulsive gambling has reached extremely high levels . . . and drugs are an instrument of death for young people. There is a global arming of drugs that is destroying this generation of young people, who are destined to be thrown away!

. . . We are throwing away our young people! Where does our future lie?

Address to the Pontifical Commission
of Latin America, February 28, 2014

Pressures of a Secular Culture

C atholic families have fewer children, with repercussions on the number of vocations to the priesthood and religious life. Some Catholics turn away from the Church to other groups who seem to promise something better. Abortion compounds the grief of many women who now carry with them deep physical and spiritual wounds after succumbing to the pressures of a secular culture which devalues God's gift of sexuality and the right to life of the unborn. In addition, the rate of separation and divorce is high, even in many Christian families, and children frequently do not grow up in a stable home environment. We also observe with great concern, and can only deplore, an increase in violence against women and children. All these realities threaten the sanctity of marriage, the stability of life in the home, and, consequently, the life of society as a whole.

... The holiness and indissolubility of Christian matrimony, often disintegrating under tremendous pressure from the secular world, must be deepened by clear doctrine and supported by the witness of committed married couples. Christian matrimony is a lifelong covenant of love between one man and one woman; it entails real sacrifices in order to turn away from illusory notions of sexual freedom and in order to foster conjugal fidelity. [Parish] programs of preparation for the sacrament of Matrimony, enriched by Pope John Paul's teaching on marriage and the family, are proving to be promising and indeed indispensable means of communicating the liberating truth about Christian marriage and are inspiring young people with new hope for themselves and for their future as husbands and wives, fathers and mothers.

Address to the Bishops of South Africa,
April 25, 2014

"Christian matrimony … entails real sacrifices in order to turn away from illusory notions of sexual freedom and in order to foster conjugal fidelity."

Look Beyond Our Boundaries

Wherever we go, even to the smallest parish in the most remote corner of this earth, there is the one Church. We are at home, we are in the family, we are among brothers and sisters. And this is a great gift of God! The Church is one for us all. There is not one Church for Europeans, one for Africans, one for Americans, one for Asians, one for those who live in Oceania. No, she is one and the same everywhere. It is like being in a family: some of its members may be far away, scattered across the world, but the deep bonds that unite all the members of a family stay solid however great the distance. I am thinking, for example, of my experience of the World Youth Day in Rio de Janeiro: in that endless crowd of young people on the beach at Copacabana we could hear many languages spoken, we could note very different facial features, we came across different cultures, and yet there was profound unity, they formed one Church, they were united and one could sense it. Let us all ask ourselves: As a Catholic, do I feel this unity? As a Catholic, do I live this unity of the Church? Or doesn't it concern me because I am closed within my own small group or within myself? Am I one of those who "privatize" the Church to their own group, their own country or their own friends? It is sad to find a "privatized" Church out of selfishness or a lack of faith. It is sad! When I hear that so many Christians in the world are suffering, am I indifferent or is it as if one of my family were suffering? When I think or hear it said that many Christians are persecuted and give their lives for their faith, does this touch my heart or not? Am I open to a brother or sister of the family who is giving his or her life for Jesus Christ? Do we pray for each other? I have a question for you, but don't answer out loud, only in your heart. How many of you pray for Christians who are being persecuted? How many? Everyone respond in your heart. Do I pray for my brother, for my sister who is in difficulty because they confess and defend their faith? It is important to look beyond our own boundaries, to feel that we are Church, one family in God!

> "When I hear that so many Christians in the world are suffering, am I indifferent or is it as if one of my family were suffering?"

General Audience, September 25, 2013

The Family's Dignity and Vocation

"The family is necessary for the survival of humanity."

Family: The World's
Driving Force

The family is a community of life which has its own autonomous consistency. As [Saint] John Paul II wrote in the Apostolic Exhortation *Familiaris Consortio*, the family is not merely the sum of persons belonging to it, but a "community of persons" (cf. nos. 17–18). And a community is more than the sum total of persons that belong to it. It is the place where one learns to love, it is the natural center of human life. It is made up of faces, of people who love, dialogue, make self-sacrifices for one another, and defend life, especially of the most vulnerable and the weakest. One could say, without exaggeration, that the family is the driving force of the world and of history. Our personality develops in the family, by growing up with our mom and dad, our brothers and sisters, by breathing in the warmth of the home. The family is the place where we receive our name, it is the place of affection, the space of intimacy, where one acquires the art of dialogue and interpersonal communication. In the family the person becomes aware of his or her own dignity and, especially if their upbringing is Christian, each one recognizes the dignity of every single person, in a particular way the sick, the weak, and the marginalized.

"One could say, without exaggeration, that the family is the driving force of the world and of history."

The family-community is all of this and it needs to be recognized as such, and more urgently today when the protection of individual rights prevail. And we must defend the right of this community: the family.

*Address to the participants in the plenary assembly
of the Pontifical Council for the Family, October 25, 2013*

Centers of Love

What is the family? Over and above its most pressing problems and its peremptory necessities, the family is a "center of love," where the law of respect and communion reigns and is able to resist the pressure of manipulation and domination from the world's "power centers." In the heart of the family, the person naturally and harmoniously blends into a human group, overcoming the false opposition between the individual and society. In the bosom of the family, no one is set apart: both the elderly and the child will be welcome here. The culture of encounter and of dialogue, openness to solidarity and transcendence, originates in the family.

For this, the family constitutes a great and "rich social resource" (cf. Benedict XVI, Encyclical Letter *Caritas in Veritate*, no. 44). In this sense I would like to highlight two primary factors: stability and fruitfulness.

Relationships based on faithful love, until death, like marriage, fatherhood, being a child or sibling, are learned and lived in the household. When these relationships form the basic fabric of a human society, they lend cohesion and consistency. It is therefore not possible to be part of a people, to feel as a neighbor, to take care of someone who is more distant and unfortunate if, in the heart of man, these fundamental relationships which give him security in openness toward others are broken.

"In facing a materialistic view of the world, the family does not reduce man to sterile utilitarianism, but offers a channel for the realization of his loftiest aspirations."

Moreover, family love is fruitful, and not only because it generates new lives, but because it broadens the horizon of existence, it creates a new world; it makes us believe, despite any discouragement and defeatism, that coexistence based on respect and trust is possible. In facing a materialistic view of the world, the family does not reduce man to sterile utilitarianism, but offers a channel for the realization of his loftiest aspirations.

Finally, I would like to tell you that, thanks to the basic experience of familial love, man also grows in his openness to God as Father. For this the Aparecida Document affirms that the family should not be considered as only the object of evangelization, but also the agent of evangelizing work (cf. nos. 432, 435). In it is reflected the image of God, who in his most profound mystery is a family and, in this manner, he allows human love to be seen as a sign and presence of divine love (Encyclical Letter *Lumen Fidei*, no. 52). Within the family, faith is absorbed together with a mother's milk. For example, that simple and spontaneous gesture of requesting a blessing, which is cherished in many of our nations, perfectly reflects the biblical conviction according to which God's blessing is passed on from father to son.

Cognizant of the fact that familial love dignifies all that makes man, giving him additional value, it is important to encourage families to cultivate healthy relationships among their own members, to know how to say "sorry," "thank you," "please" to each other and to address God using the beautiful name of Father.

May Our Lady of Guadalupe obtain abundant blessings from God for America's families and make them fonts of life, harmony, and robust faith, nourished by the Gospel and by good works. I ask you, please, to pray for me, because I need it.

Message to the First Latin American Congress
on the Pastoral Care of the Family Panama,
August 4–9, 2014

Illuminated by the Gospel

The "Good News" of the family is a very important part of evangelization, which Christians can communicate to all, by the witness of their lives; and already they are doing so, this is evident in secularized societies; truly Christian families are known by their fidelity, their patience, their openness to life, and by their respect for the elderly . . . the secret to this is the presence of Jesus in the family. Let us therefore propose to all people, with respect and courage, the beauty of marriage and the family illuminated by the Gospel! And in order to do this let us approach with care and affection those families who are struggling, forced to leave their homeland, broken, homeless or unemployed, or suffering for any reason; let us approach married couples in crisis or separated. Let us be close to everyone through the proclamation of this Gospel of the family, the beauty of the family.

Address to the participants in the plenary assembly
of the Pontifical Council for the Family, October 25, 2013

The Foundation of Society

L et us all work for that word which is unpopular today: solidarity. It is a word that people always try to put aside, because it is irksome, and yet it is a word that reflects the human and Christian values that are required of us today . . . so as to counter the throwaway culture, according to which everything is disposable. A culture that always leaves people out of the equation: it leaves children out, it leaves young people out, it leaves the elderly out, it leaves out all who are of no use, who do not produce, and this must not be!

Not only would I say that the family is important for the evangelization of the new world. The family is important, and it is necessary for the survival of humanity. Without the family, the cultural survival of the human race would be at risk. The family, whether we like it or not, is the foundation.

Interview for the radio of the Archdiocese of Rio, July 27, 2013

The Fundamental Cell

The family is experiencing a profound cultural crisis, as are all communities and social bonds. In the case of the family, the weakening of these bonds is particularly serious because the family is the fundamental cell of society, where we learn to live with others despite our differences and to belong to one another; it is also the place where parents pass on the faith to their children. Marriage now tends to be viewed as a form of mere emotional satisfaction that can be constructed in any way or modified at will. But the indispensible contribution of marriage to society transcends the feelings and momentary needs of the couple. As the French bishops have taught, it is not born "of loving sentiment, ephemeral by definition, but from the depth of the obligation assumed by the spouses who accept to enter a total communion of life."

The individualism of our postmodern and globalized era favors a lifestyle which weakens the development and stability of personal relationships and distorts family bonds. Pastoral activity needs to bring out more clearly the fact that our relationship with the Father demands and encourages a communion which heals, promotes, and reinforces interpersonal bonds. In our world, especially in some countries, different forms of war and conflict are re-emerging, yet we Christians remain steadfast in our intention to respect others, to heal wounds, to build bridges, to strengthen relationships, and to "bear one another's burdens" (Gal 6:2).

Apostolic Exhortation Evangelii Gaudium
(nos. 66–67), November 24, 2013

A Privileged Place
for Evangelization

"The Christian family, in fact, is the first community called to announce the Gospel to the human person during growth and to bring him or her, through a progressive education and catechesis, to full human and Christian maturity" (*Familiaris Consortio*, no. 2). Marital fidelity is above all the foundation upon which a harmonious family life can be built. Unfortunately, in our time, we see that the family and marriage are undergoing a deep inner crisis in the countries of the Western world. "In the case of the family, the weakening of these bonds is particularly serious because the family is the fundamental cell of society, where we learn to live with others despite our differences and to belong to one another; it is also the place where parents pass on the faith to their children" (*Evangelii Gaudium*, no. 66). Globalization and postmodern individualism promote a lifestyle that makes it much more difficult to develop stable bonds between people, and it is not conducive to promoting a culture of the family. This opens up a new mission field for the Church, for example, among groups of families where opportunities are created for interpersonal relationships and for a relationship with God, where authentic communion that welcomes everyone equally can grow, that does not close itself off into groups of the élite, that heals wounds, builds bridges, goes in search of the lost, and helps "to bear one another's burdens" (Gal 6:2).

> "The family, therefore, is a privileged place for evangelization and the living transmission of the faith."

The family, therefore, is a privileged place for evangelization and the living transmission of the faith. Let us do everything possible to ensure that our families pray and experience and transmit the faith as an integral part of daily life. The Church's concern for the family begins with the proper preparation and appropriate support of spouses, as well as the faithful and clear explanation of the Church's doctrine on marriage and on the family. Sacramental marriage is a gift of God as well as a commitment. The love of two spouses is sanctified by Christ, and a married couple is called to bear witness to and cultivate this sanctity through their faithful love for one another.

Address to the Bishops of Austria, January 30, 2014

Weaving Together
the Story of Life

It is significant how—even in the individualistic culture which distorts bonds and renders them ephemeral—in each person born of woman there remains alive an essential need for stability, for an open door, for someone with whom to weave and to share the story of life, a history to belong to. The communion of life embraced by spouses, their openness to the gift of life, the mutual protection, the encounter and the memory of generations, educational support, the transmission of the Christian faith to their children. . . . With all this, the family continues to be a school unparalleled in humanity, an indispensable contribution to a just and supportive society (cf. Apostolic Exhortation *Evangelii Gaudium*, nos. 66–68). And the deeper its roots, the more possible it is in life to go out and go far, without getting lost or feeling a stranger in a foreign land.

. . . Our *listening* and our *discussion* on the family, loved with the *gaze* of Christ, will become a providential occasion with which to renew . . . the Church and society. With the joy of the Gospel we will rediscover the way of a reconciled and merciful Church, poor and a friend of the poor; a Church "given strength that it might, in patience and in love, overcome its sorrows and its challenges, both within itself and from without" (*Lumen Gentium*, no. 8).

Address during the Meeting on the Family, October 4, 2014

Passing on the Faith

*"How precious is the family as the privileged place
for transmitting the faith!"*

Links in a Chain

Jesus did not need to be baptized, but the first theologians say that, with his body, with his divinity, in baptism he blessed all the waters, so that the waters would have the power to confer baptism. And then, before ascending to heaven, Jesus told us to go into all the world to baptize. And from that day forward up until today, this has been an uninterrupted chain: they baptized their children, and their children their own, and those children. . . . And also today this chain continues.

These children are a link in a chain. You parents have a baby boy or girl to baptize, but in some years they will have a child to baptize, or a grandchild. . . . Such is the chain of faith! What does this mean? I would like to tell you only this: you are those who transmit the faith, the transmitters; you have a duty to hand on the faith to these children. It is the most beautiful inheritance you will leave to them: the faith! Only this. Today, take this thought home with you. We must be transmitters of the faith. Think about this, always think about how to hand on the faith to your children.

Today the choir sings, but the most beautiful choir is the children making noise . . . Some of them will cry, because they are uncomfortable or because they are hungry: if they are hungry, Mothers, feed them with ease, because they are the most important ones here.

Homily, January 12, 2014

The Power of the Holy Spirit

The word "Confirmation" . . . reminds us that this sacrament brings an increase and deepening of baptismal grace; it unites us more firmly to Christ, it renders our bond with the Church more perfect, and it gives us a special strength of the Holy Spirit to spread and defend the faith . . . to confess the name of Christ boldly, and never to be ashamed of his cross (cf. *Catechism of the Catholic Church*, no. 1303).

For this reason, it is important to take care that our children, our young people, receive this sacrament. We all take care that they are baptized and this is good, but perhaps we do not take so much care to ensure that they are confirmed. Thus they remain at a midpoint in their journey and do not receive the Holy Spirit, who is so important in the Christian life since he gives us the strength to go on. Let us think a little, each one of us: Do we truly care whether our children, our young people, receive Confirmation? This is important, it is important! And if you have children or adolescents at home who have not yet received it and are at the age to do so, do everything possible to ensure that they complete their Christian initiation and receive the power of the Holy Spirit. It is important!

Naturally it is important to prepare those being confirmed well, leading them toward a personal commitment to faith in Christ and reawakening in them a sense of belonging to the Church.

Confirmation, like every sacrament, is not the work of men but of God, who cares for our lives in such a manner as to mold us in the image of his Son, to make us capable of loving like him. He does it by infusing in us his Holy Spirit, whose action pervades the whole person and his entire life, as reflected in the seven gifts that Tradition, in light of Sacred Scripture, has always highlighted. These seven gifts—I do not want to ask you if you remember the seven gifts. Perhaps you will all know them. . . . But I will say them on your behalf. What are these gifts? Wisdom, understanding, counsel, fortitude, knowledge, piety, and fear of the Lord. And these gifts have been given to us precisely with the Holy Spirit in the sacrament of Confirmation. I therefore intend to dedicate the catecheses that follow those on the sacrament to these seven gifts.

When we welcome the Holy Spirit into our hearts and allow him to act, Christ makes himself present in us and takes shape in our lives; through us, it will be he—Christ himself—who prays,

> "When we welcome the Holy Spirit into our hearts and allow him to act, Christ makes himself present in us and takes shape in our lives . . ."

forgives, gives hope and consolation, serves the brethren, draws close to the needy and to the least, creates community, and sows peace. Think how important this is: by means of the Holy Spirit, Christ himself comes to do all this among us and for us. That is why it is important that children and young people receive the Sacrament of Confirmation.

General Audience, January 29, 2014

Giving Away the Faith

The family keeps the faith. The Apostle Paul, at the end of his life, makes a final reckoning and says: "I have kept the faith" (2 Tim 4:7). But how did he keep the faith? Not in a strong box! Nor did he hide it underground, like the somewhat lazy servant. Saint Paul compares his life to a fight and to a race. He kept the faith because he didn't just defend it, but proclaimed it, spread it, brought it to distant lands. He stood up to all those who wanted to preserve, to "embalm" the message of Christ within the limits of Palestine. That is why he made courageous decisions, went into hostile territory, let himself be challenged by distant peoples and different cultures, spoke frankly and fearlessly. Saint Paul kept the faith because, in the same way that he received it, he gave it away, he went out to the fringes and didn't dig himself into defensive positions.

Here, too, we can ask: How do we keep our faith as a family? Do we keep it for ourselves, in our families, as a personal treasure like a bank account, or are we able to share it by our witness, by our acceptance of others, by our openness? We all know that families, especially young families, are often "racing" from one place to another, with lots to do. But did you ever think that this "racing" could also be the race of faith? Christian families are missionary families. Yesterday in this square we heard the testimonies of missionary families. They are missionary also in everyday life, in their doing everyday things, as they bring to everything the salt and the leaven of faith! Keeping the faith in families and bringing to everyday things the salt and the leaven of faith.

> "Christian families are missionary families."

Homily, October 27, 2013

We Do Not Find Faith
in the Abstract

I had the great blessing of growing up in a family in which faith was lived in a simple, practical way. However, it was my paternal grandmother in particular who influenced my journey of faith. She was a woman who explained to us, who talked to us about Jesus, who taught us the catechism. I always remember that on the evening of Good Friday she would take us to the candlelight procession, and at the end of this procession "the dead Christ" would arrive and our grandmother would make us—the children—kneel down and she would say to us: "Look, he is dead, but tomorrow he will rise." This was how I received my first Christian proclamation, from this very woman, from my grandmother! This is really beautiful! The first proclamation at home, in the family! And this makes me think of the love of so many mothers and grandmothers in the transmission of faith. They are the ones who pass on the faith. This used to happen in the early

Church too, for Saint Paul said to Timothy: "I am reminded of the faith of your mother and of your grandmother" (cf. 2 Tim 1:5). All the mothers and all the grandmothers who are here should think about this: passing on the faith! Because God sets beside us people who help us on our journey of faith. We do not find our faith in the abstract, no! It is always a person preaching who tells us who Jesus is, who communicates faith to us and gives us the

> "It is always a person preaching who tells us who Jesus is, who communicates faith to us and gives us the first proclamation."

first proclamation. And this is how I received my first experience of faith.

Address on the Vigil of Pentecost, May 18, 2013

The Essential Witness
of Women

In the profession of faith in the New Testament only men are recorded as witnesses of the Resurrection, the Apostles, but not the women. This is because, according to the Judaic Law of that time, women and children could not bear a trustworthy, credible witness. Instead in the Gospels women play a fundamental lead role. Here we can grasp an element in favor of the historicity of the Resurrection: If it was an invented event, in the context of that time it would not have been linked with the evidence of women. Instead the Evangelists simply recounted what happened: women were the first witnesses. This implies that God does not choose in accordance with human criteria: the first witnesses of the birth of Jesus were shepherds, simple, humble people; the first witnesses of the Resurrection were women. And this is beautiful. This is part of the mission of women; of mothers, of women! Witnessing to their children, to their grandchildren, that Jesus is alive, is living, is risen. Mothers and women, carry on witnessing to this! It is the heart that counts for God, how open to him we are, whether we are like trusting children.

However, this also makes us think about how women, in the Church and on the journey of faith, had and still have today a special role in opening the doors to the Lord, in following him and in communicating his Face, for the gaze of faith is always in need of the simple and profound gaze of love.

General Audience, April 3, 2013

Like a River That Irrigates

As from generation to generation life is transmitted, so too from generation to generation, through rebirth at the baptismal font, grace is transmitted, and by this grace the Christian people journeys through time, like a river that irrigates the land and spreads God's blessing throughout the world. From the moment that Jesus said what we heard in the Gospel reading, the disciples went out to baptize; and from that time until today there is a chain in the transmission of the faith through Baptism. And each one of us is a link in that chain: a step forward, always, like a river that irrigates. Such is the grace of God and such is our faith, which we must transmit to our sons and daughters, transmit to children, so that once adults, they can do the same for their children. This is what Baptism is. Why? Because Baptism lets us enter this People of God that transmits the faith. This is very important. A People of God that journeys and hands down the faith. . . .

On the subject of the importance of Baptism for the People of God, the history of the *Christian community in Japan* is exemplary. It suffered severe persecution at the start of the seventeenth century. There were many martyrs, members of the clergy were expelled and thousands of faithful killed. No priest was left in Japan, they were all expelled. Then the community retreated into hiding, keeping the faith and prayer in seclusion. And when a child was born, the father or mother baptized him or her, because the faithful can baptize in certain circumstances. When, after roughly two and a half centuries, 250 years later, missionaries returned to Japan, thousands of Christians stepped out into the open and the Church was able to flourish again. They survived by the grace of Baptism! This is profound: the People of God transmits the faith, baptizes her children, and goes forward. And they maintained, even in secret, a strong communal spirit, because their Baptism had made of them one single body in Christ: they were isolated and hidden, but they were always members of the People of God, members of the Church. Let us learn a great deal from this history!

> "And each one of us is a link in that chain: a step forward, always, like a river that irrigates."

Angelus message, January 15, 2014

Keeping Jesus Alive
in the Church

The Eucharistic Celebration is much more than simple banquet: it is exactly the memorial of Jesus' Paschal Sacrifice, the mystery at the center of salvation. "Memorial" does not simply mean a remembrance, a mere memory; it means that every time we celebrate this sacrament we participate in the mystery of the passion, death, and resurrection of Christ. The Eucharist is the summit of God's saving action: the Lord Jesus, by becoming bread broken for us, pours upon us all his mercy and his love, so as to renew our hearts, our lives, and our way of relating with him and with the brethren. It is for this reason that commonly, when we approach this sacrament, we speak of "receiving Communion," of "taking Communion": this means that by the power of the Holy Spirit, participation in Holy Communion conforms us in a singular and profound way to Christ, giving us a foretaste already now of the full communion with the Father that characterizes the heavenly banquet, where together with all the saints we will have the joy of contemplating God face to face.

Dear friends, we don't ever thank the Lord enough for the gift he has given us in the Eucharist! It is a very great gift and that is why it is so important to go to Mass on Sunday. Go to Mass not just to pray, but to receive Communion, the bread that is the Body of Jesus Christ who saves us, forgives us, unites us to the Father. It is a beautiful thing to do! And we go to Mass every Sunday because that is the day of the resurrection of the Lord. That is why Sunday is so important to us. And in this Eucharist we feel this belonging to the Church, to the People of God, to the Body of God, to Jesus Christ. We will never completely grasp the value and the richness of it. Let us ask him then that this Sacrament continue to keep his presence alive in the Church and to shape our community in charity and communion, according to the Father's heart. This is done throughout life, but is begun on the day of our First Communion. It is important that children be prepared well for their First Communion and that every child receive it, because it is the first step of this intense belonging to Jesus Christ, after Baptism and Confirmation.

> "... the Lord Jesus, by becoming bread broken for us, pours upon us all of his mercy and his love, so as to renew our hearts, our lives, and our way of relating with him and with the brethren."

General Audience, February 5, 2014

Transmitting
Not Only Content

We repeatedly hear the phrase: *transmission of the faith*; the expression is not so surprising. We know that nowadays it is a real must; how is the faith to be transmitted, this was the theme of the previous Synod on evangelization. *Educational emergency* is an expression which you recently adopted together with those who have prepared this work. And I like it, because it makes room for anthropology, an anthropological vision of evangelization, an anthropological foundation for it. If there is an educational emergency with regard to the transmission of the faith, it is how to address the issue of catechizing young people from the perspective—we might say—of fundamental theology. In other words, what are the anthropological presuppositions present today in the transmission of the faith that have led to this educational emergency for the youth of Latin America? For this, I believe we need to reiterate and return to the great criteria of education.

And the first criterion of education is that it is . . . not only about imparting knowledge and transmitting content. It involves multiple dimensions: the transmission of *content*, *habits*, and a *sense of values*—these three things together.

> "Transmitting the faith requires forming habits of behavior; one must create the proper conditions for young people to receive the values that will prepare them, and enable these habits to grow . . ."

Transmitting the faith requires forming habits of behavior; one must create the proper conditions for young people to receive the values that will prepare them, and enable these habits to grow; and then one needs to provide basic content. Were we to transmit the faith by content alone, its reception would be merely superficial or ideological and without roots. Transmission of faith must be about content and values, together with a sense of values and habits, habits of behavior. The old suggestions that our confessors made when we were boys: "So this week do this, this, and this . . . " were meant to instill in us a habit of behavior; not only content, but also values. The transmission of the faith should be framed in this way.

Address to the Pontifical Commission of Latin America, February 28, 2014

Every Disciple Is a Missionary

The Church's intimacy with Jesus is an itinerant intimacy; it presumes that we step out of ourselves, that we walk and sow again and again, in an ever wider radius. The Lord said, "Let us go to the nearby villages to preach, for this is why I have come." It is vital for the Church not to close in on herself, not to feel satisfied and secure with what she has achieved. If this were to happen the Church would fall ill, ill of an imaginary abundance, of superfluous abundance; in a certain way, she would "get indigestion" and be weakened. We need to go forth from our own communities and be bold enough to go to the existential outskirts that need to feel the closeness of God. He abandons no one, and he always shows his unfailing tenderness and mercy; this, therefore, is what we need to take to all people. . . .

Remember that you have been baptized, that you have been transformed into the Lord's disciples. But every disciple is also a missionary. Benedict XVI said they are two sides to the same coin. I beg you, as your father and brother in Jesus Christ, to take care of the faith you received in Baptism. And, like the mother and grandmother of Timothy, hand on the faith to your children and grandchildren, and not only to them. This treasure of faith is not given for our own personal use. It is meant to be given, to be handed on, and in this way it grows. Make the name of Jesus known.

Video Message to the Pilgrimage-Meeting at the Shrine of Our Lady of Guadalupe, November 16, 2013

BOOKS & MEDIA

A mission of the Daughters of St. Paul

As apostles of Jesus Christ, evangelizing today's world:

We are CALLED to holiness
by God's living Word and Eucharist.

We COMMUNICATE the Gospel message
through our lives and through all
available forms of media.

We SERVE the Church
by responding to the hopes and needs
of all people with the Word of God,
in the spirit of St. Paul.

For more information visit our Web site:
www.pauline.org.

Pauline
BOOKS & MEDIA

The Daughters of St. Paul operate book and media centers at the following addresses. Visit, call, or write the one nearest you today, or find us at www.paulinestore.org.

CALIFORNIA

3908 Sepulveda Blvd, Culver City, CA 90230 — 310-397-8676

3250 Middlefield Road, Menlo Park, CA 94025 — 650-369-4230

FLORIDA

145 S.W. 107th Avenue, Miami, FL 33174 — 305-559-6715

HAWAII

1143 Bishop Street, Honolulu, HI 96813 — 808-521-2731

ILLINOIS

172 North Michigan Avenue, Chicago, IL 60601 — 312-346-4228

LOUISIANA

4403 Veterans Memorial Blvd, Metairie, LA 70006 — 504-887-7631

MASSACHUSETTS

885 Providence Hwy, Dedham, MA 02026 — 781-326-5385

MISSOURI

9804 Watson Road, St. Louis, MO 63126 — 314-965-3512

NEW YORK

64 W. 38th Street, New York, NY 10018 — 212-754-1110

SOUTH CAROLINA

243 King Street, Charleston, SC 29401 — 843-577-0175

TEXAS

Currently no book center; for parish exhibits or outreach evangelization, contact: 210-569-0500, or SanAntonio@paulinemedia.com, or P.O. Box 761416, San Antonio, TX 78245

VIRGINIA

1025 King Street, Alexandria, VA 22314 — 703-549-3806

CANADA

3022 Dufferin Street, Toronto, ON M6B 3T5 — 416-781-9131

¡También somos su fuente para libros,
videos y música en español!